HEROES OF HISTORY

CLARA BARTON

Courage under Fire

I0896003

HEROES OF HISTORY

CLARA BARTON

Courage under Fire

JANET & GEOFF BENGE

Emerald Books

P.O. BOX 635, LYNNWOOD, WA 98046

Emerald Books are distributed through YWAM Publishing. For a full list of titles, including other great biographies, visit our website at www.ywampublishing.com or call 1-800-922-2143.

Clara Barton: Courage under Fire

Published by Emerald Books
P.O. Box 635
Lynnwood, Washington 98046

Library of Congress Cataloging-in-Publication Data
Benge, Janet, 1958–
Clara Barton : courage under fire / by Janet and Geoff Benge.
p. cm. — (Heroes of history)
American Red Cross.
Includes bibliographical references.
ISBN 1-883002-50-8
1. Barton, Clara, 1821–1912—Juvenile literature. 2. Red Cross—United States—Biography—Juvenile literature. 3. Nurses—United States—Biography—Juvenile literature. [1. Barton, Clara, 1821–1912. 2. Nurses. 3. American National Red Cross. 4. Women—Biography.] I. Benge, Geoff, 1954– II. Title.
HV569.B3 B45 2002
361.7'634'092—dc21 2002014066

ISBN-13: 978-1-883002-50-3
ISBN-10: 1-883002-50-8

Fifth printing 2021

Printed in the United States of America

HEROES OF HISTORY

Biographies

Abraham Lincoln
Alan Shepard
Ben Carson
Benjamin Franklin
Benjamin Rush
Billy Graham
Captain John Smith
Christopher Columbus
Clara Barton
Davy Crockett
Daniel Boone
Douglas MacArthur
Elizabeth Fry
Ernest Shackleton
George Washington
George Washington Carver
Harriet Tubman
John Adams
Laura Ingalls Wilder
Louis Zamperini
Meriwether Lewis
Milton Hershey
Orville Wright
Ronald Reagan
Theodore Roosevelt
Thomas Edison
William Bradford
William Penn
William Wilberforce

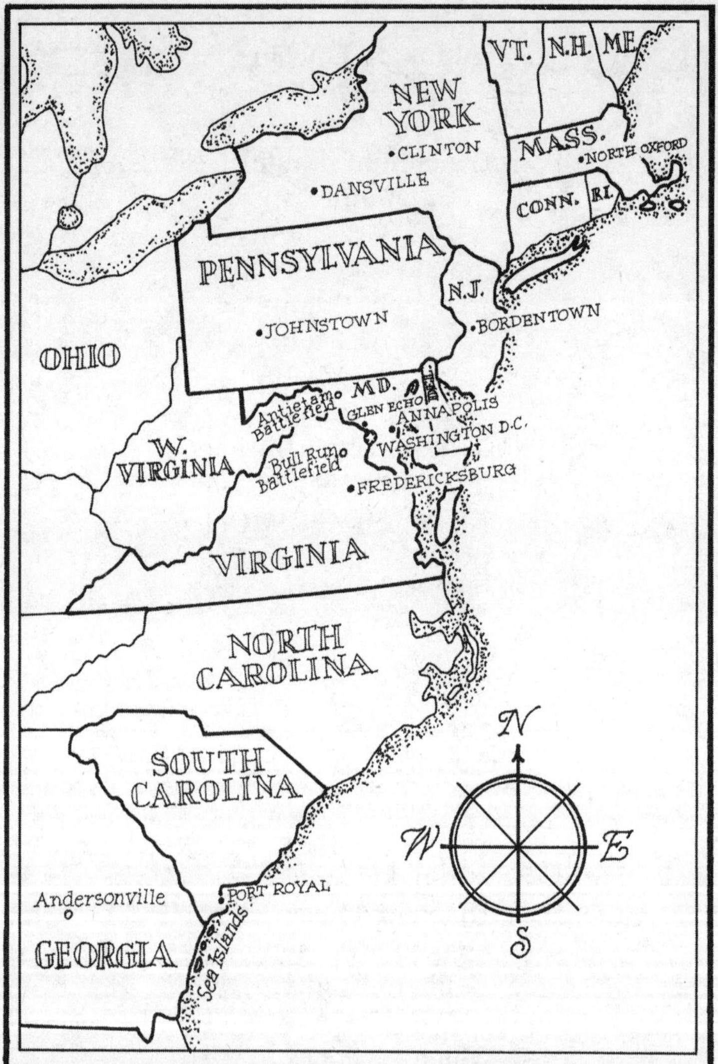

VT.
N.H.
ME.
NEW YORK
CLINTON
DANSVILLE
MASS.
NORTH OXFORD
CONN.
R.I.
PENNSYLVANIA
N.J.
BORDENTOWN
JOHNSTOWN
OHIO
MD.
Antietam Battlefield
GLEN ECHO
ANNAPOLIS
WASHINGTON D.C.
W. VIRGINIA
Bull Run Battlefield
FREDERICKSBURG
VIRGINIA
NORTH CAROLINA
SOUTH CAROLINA
N
W
E
S
Andersonville
PORT ROYAL
GEORGIA
Sea Islands

Contents

Chapter 1

Over the River

Clara Barton grabbed a wad of cotton and held it to the soldier's face—or what was left of it. Half of it was a gaping hole, blown away by a bullet.

"As soon as we stop the bleeding, we'll get you to the hospital," Clara said in her soothing voice. The soldier looked into her eyes and nodded.

Just then a messenger arrived at the aid station. Clara was the only woman there, and the messenger made a beeline for her. He handed her a bloodstained note, which she unfolded quickly and read. "Come to me. Your place is here. Dr. Cutter."

"Where is Dr. Cutter?" Clara asked the messenger.

"In the thick of the fighting over the river in Fredericksburg, ma'am," he replied.

"Then I shall go to him immediately," Clara said.

As Clara spoke, George, her assistant, grabbed her hand. His voice was thick with urgency. "You cannot cross the Rappahannock!" he exclaimed. "Let me go in your place."

Clara smiled at him. He had become a loyal friend. "George, I must go. The doctor has asked for me. You cannot go in my place, but you can go with me if you like."

"Yes, ma'am," George replied. "I certainly would."

Soon the two of them were picking their way across the pontoon bridge to the other side of the Rappahannock River. Shells exploded in the water around them, soaking the wood and making it treacherously slippery. Clara proved as surefooted as the men who were marching past her. She was grateful for all the balancing games she had played on logs at her brothers' sawmill when she was a child.

When they reached the far side of the river, a Union soldier helped Clara onto the shore. She heard a deafening whiz as a piece of exploding shell flew past her, clipping her skirt, and burned a hole in the soldier's coat. She took a deep breath and then asked the soldier where Dr. Cutter was.

"Over there, in that two-story house with the green trim," he replied. "I hope you make it up there in one piece. I am sorry I cannot accompany you, but I have been stationed here at the bridge."

"I will be all right," Clara replied as she and George started walking up the hill.

George had already crossed the street when a regiment of Union soldiers marched into view. Clara stopped to wait for them to pass. An elderly colonel drew his horse to a halt beside her. "You are alone and in great danger, ma'am," he yelled. "Do you want protection?"

Clara smiled up at him. He obviously thought she was a woman from Fredericksburg who had not noticed that a war was being fought in her front yard!

"Thank you very much," she replied, "but I believe I am the best-protected woman in the United States."

When the soldiers nearest to Clara heard what she said, they cried, "That's so! That's so! Three cheers for Miss Barton!" Soon a cheer echoed all the way down the ranks. It appeared the colonel was the only one who had not realized who she was. He bowed his head and tipped his hat. "I believe you are right," he said before galloping off.

Clara stood there for a moment. She wished her father could see her now, plunging into the jaws of the Battle of Fredericksburg! Even she could hardly believe how she had changed from a timid young girl into a woman who risked her life for the sake of caring for wounded Union soldiers. It had been quite a journey from the family farm in North Oxford, Massachusetts, to this Civil War battlefield.

Chapter 2

A Shy Little Girl

Boom. They're all dead!" Captain Stephen Barton exclaimed and then added, "You should have done a better job at protecting your left flank."

"But I needed the cavalry over here. I was going to attack your infantrymen," Clara replied indignantly as she looked at the "battle scene" spread out on the rug she and her father were sitting on.

She often played war games with her father, a veteran of the Revolutionary War. They used corn seeds for the infantry, dried peas for the cavalry, and tiny twigs to represent cannons.

At three years of age, Clara had no idea that this was not the kind of game most little girls played in 1824. This was because she never played with other children. The world she lived in was one filled with adults. And even if some of them were her brothers and sisters, they seemed much more like extra sets of parents to her.

There was Dorothy, or Dolly, as everyone called her. She was a twenty-year-old schoolteacher who spent her free moments embroidering and writing poetry. Stephen was next; he was nineteen and also a schoolteacher. His favorite subject was mathematics, and he often made Clara do sums and count coins. David was seventeen years old and Clara's hero. Although he was two years younger than Stephen, he was bigger and stronger. He and Clara shared a love of animals, and Clara constantly pestered him to teach her how to ride a horse. Her fourteen-year-old sister, blonde and beautiful Sally, was closest in age, but even she seemed ancient to Clara. Each sibling took a special interest in Clara that made her feel as though she had not only six parents, but also six teachers.

Clara had a good memory and was able to learn easily. She had already memorized the names of all six past presidents and vice presidents of the United States, and Dolly and Stephen brought spelling and reading books home from school for her to learn from. In addition Clara knew many of her father's war stories by heart. Her favorite story, which she begged to hear every night, was about how, after a battle, Captain Barton had been left behind in the marshlands of Michigan, too ill to move. He nearly died of thirst before a rainstorm left a puddle of water in a horse's hoofprint near him. He drank from the puddle and was soon strong enough to lure a stray dog, which he killed and ate and so was able to survive and make it to safety.

Clara's birthday fell on Christmas Day, and soon after she was four years old, everyone agreed she should start school. On her first day, Stephen threw her up onto his shoulders and set out in the snow. As Stephen walked, Clara turned to look back at the compact, one-and-a-half story New England farmhouse where she had lived all her life. The house was located on the top of a rise in the small farming community of North Oxford, Massachusetts. She gulped as she watched her mother and sisters waving goodbye from the doorway. It was the first time she would be left with strangers, and she was not looking forward to the experience.

Clara also felt very self-conscious about her hair. Her mother, Sarah Stone Barton, was never one to fuss over little girls. She made it clear that she could not be bothered grooming her daughter's thick, long, brown hair. The day before, she had clipped Clara's hair short like a boy's. Clara was mortified. Her long ringlets were gone. She looked like a newly shorn sheep.

It was about a mile through the snowdrifts to the one-room schoolhouse. Clara clung to Stephen as he introduced her to the teacher. "Say hello to Mr. Stone," Stephen urged her, but she could not find her voice, and only a squeak came out.

Stephen laughed, but Mr. Stone kept quiet, his soft eyes welcoming her. Slowly Clara relaxed enough for Stephen to pry her fingers free from the grip she had of his trousers. "Be good, and I'll come back for you at three," he said.

Clara nodded and looked around. The schoolhouse was filled with over fifty children. She recognized some of them from church and others from barn raisings and various community events, but she did not know any of them well. Nor did she know how to go about making friends with the other children. In fact, the only person in the room she felt she could relate to was Mr. Stone, the teacher.

"Come on over here, Clara," Mr. Stone said. "How old are you?"

"Four years old," she replied with her characteristic lisp.

"Well, then, I'm sure you belong in the front row with the other beginners. Some of them may be a little ahead of you, but I'll help you catch up."

Mr. Stone placed a reader in front of her. "Tell me, do you recognize any letters or words here?" he asked.

Clara took one look at the page and indignation rose within her. These were baby words! *Dog* and *cat* and *go*. Dolly and Stephen had taught her these words over a year ago! She was up to the third-grade list—the list that started with the word *artichoke*.

Suddenly terror seized Clara. Either she had to tell Mr. Stone that she could read, or she was going to be stuck with children who were way behind her. She felt her heart race and her mouth go dry. The thought of coming to school and not learning anything new urged her on. She spoke up. "Sir, I know all the words in this list, and the grade-two list as well. I am up to grade three. You know, the list that begins with *artichoke*."

Clara watched as a bemused smile spread over Mr. Stone's face. "Are you now?" he replied. "Thank you for telling me. It wouldn't do for an artichoke girl to be stuck with the dogs and cats now, would it?"

"No, it would not," Clara agreed, relieved that he believed her. She was soon sitting three rows back with children who were much older than she, but who she decided were not nearly as smart.

Clara started her work with great enthusiasm, even writing her full name—Clarissa Harlowe Barton—at the top of the page. She had been named after her Aunt Clarissa, but somehow the full name never stuck, and the only name she could remember being called was Clara.

It took several weeks before the terrible knot in Clara's stomach untied itself, and eventually she got used to school and the other students. She seldom played with the others, though, and they left her alone to work, which she was grateful for.

The thing Clara liked most about school was the way Mr. Stone tried to find interesting things to teach her. She loved to study the huge map of the world that hung in the corner, and so her teacher introduced her to a fourth-grade geography book. She took the book home and studied it at every opportunity. Sometimes Clara even woke before the sun was up and studied the book by candlelight. The exotic names of rivers, mountain ranges, countries, and oceans fired her imagination, and she decided she would visit some of these places one day.

Once Clara had settled into school, she was sure she was big enough to learn to ride. She finally convinced David to take her out on Billy, an unbroken colt. David hoisted his sister onto the colt's back. Clara grabbed the animal's mane and held on with all her strength. No sooner was she on his back than the colt bolted, kicking his hind legs into the air, trying to dislodge her before galloping at full speed across the open field toward a group of other colts. Despite the best efforts of the colt, Clara stayed perched on his back, her knuckles white from grasping his mane. Finally the animal realized he had lost the fight and stopped trying to buck her off. Horse and rider then galloped up and down the field until David caught up to them and helped his little sister to the ground.

Despite the fact that Clara was short for her age, she soon became a competent and fearless horse rider, which was strange, considering all of the other things she was scared of. Thunder and lightning sent her diving under the bed, and when she saw a snake on the veranda, she refused to go outside for days.

When she was six years old, another event scared Clara. It happened to her then twenty-three-year-old sister Dolly, and it scared Clara so much that she dared not even ask about it. Dolly had always been interested in Clara's life, and she taught her youngest sister many things. But slowly Clara noticed a difference in her oldest sister. Dolly often sat staring at the fire and would not answer when she was spoken to. One night Clara watched in horror as Dolly cut to shreds the embroidered pillow she had just finished. And there was the time when Dolly had rocked on the rocking chair so hard that it tipped over, and then she lay there on the floor muttering to herself.

Clara also noticed that the other adults in the house held conversations in quiet voices and became silent when she entered the room. Eventually Captain Barton put bars on the windows in Dolly's bedroom and Dolly was kept in her room with the door locked. Clara understood that something had gone seriously wrong with her big sister's mind, though she could not grasp exactly what it was. No one could, and since there was no treatment for mental illness, the family learned to live with Dolly's screams and pleas.

All this frightened Clara a great deal, and she wondered whether the same thing would happen to her when she grew older, though she dared not discuss her fears with anyone. Sometimes Dolly seemed a little better and she was allowed downstairs to talk to the family and help with simple chores, though she never left the house.

About this time, Stephen left schoolteaching and partnered with David in opening a sawmill, appropriately named S & D Barton Mills. The French River wound its way through New Oxford, and the waterwheels along it were used to power a number of flour mills and sawmills. Clara loved to go down to the mill and climb about on the huge logs and the machines that hauled the logs onto the saw bed.

Clara knew that her parents were very proud of her older brothers, and she tried hard to make them proud of her as well. The only problem was that whatever she did, some other member of the family had already done much better years before. Still, she toiled on, learning all she could and spending her free time outdoors riding Billy or running in the hills with her white terrier, Buttons. She seldom had to do much housework, because her mother had most of it done before Clara got up. Mrs. Barton had a lot of trouble sleeping, and so she got up at 3 A.M. each morning and started on the household chores. By sunup the laundry was already boiled and scrubbed and the floors shone to a high polish. This was fine with Clara; she would rather be outdoors playing than doing chores inside.

Life took an unexpected turn for Clara when she was eight years old. She overheard a conversation between her parents. The door to their bedroom was open, and something made her stop and listen to what was being said.

"She's not going to get more outgoing on her own," Clara heard her mother say sharply. "We have to do something to force her to make friends or she's never going to."

"Oh, I don't know," Clara's father replied, "It seems like a huge step to send her to boarding school. Maybe Clara will just grow more confident in her own time."

"Now, Stephen, that's what you said when she started school, and just the other day the teacher told me that Clara hangs around him at recess and has very little to do with the other children. I say we do something."

Clara's heart lurched as she realized they were talking about her—and boarding school! She wanted to storm into her parents' bedroom and tell them that she would not go, but she dared not take such a bold action.

Later that night Clara's father called her aside and broke the news she already knew and dreaded. Mr. Stone had opened a boarding school nearby, and Clara was to be sent there. Her father told her that he hoped she would be a good girl and go along with the plan and that since she would see Mr. Stone every day, it would not be too bad.

The buggy ride to boarding school was long and lonely. Clara sat beside her father, but she was too worried to talk. By the time they got to the school, she was in a terrible state. She froze when she saw the other children, and even Mr. Stone's kindness did nothing to reassure her. That night as she lay in bed, all she could think of was what her family was doing and where Buttons would sleep without his mistress.

The next day Clara sat down for meals with the other children, but although the food smelled good, she could not bring herself to eat a single bite. And she couldn't eat the following day or the day after that either. Finally, after two weeks, she was gaunt and thin. Her eyes were swollen from crying, and she could not concentrate on her schoolwork.

It was a wonderful relief to Clara when one day her father showed up. He took one look at her and his eyes grew wide. "What's the matter with you, Clara?" he asked softly.

Clara burst into tears. "I want to go home. Please take me home."

Captain Barton scooped Clara up into his arms and hugged her tight. She could smell the familiar scent of the farmhouse on his coat. "I'll take you home," he whispered in her ear, "and you'll never have to leave again unless you want to."

On the trip home, Clara felt as if she had been liberated from prison. She could not wait to sleep in her own bed and ride Billy with Buttons running along behind. Surely now everything would get back to normal.

Chapter 3

Accidents

"Clara, I have something to tell you," Captain Barton said one night after the family had finished dinner. Sally and her mother were in the kitchen washing the dishes.

"What is it?" Clara asked in a husky voice. She could tell from her father's tone that he had something important to tell her. She just hoped it did not involve any more changes in the family.

Captain Barton went on. "I don't suppose you know, but Jeremiah's widow, Eliza, has been struggling with the farm ever since he died."

Clara nodded. She recalled when her older cousin Jeremiah Learned had died and how awkward it had been trying to think of something to say to his four children.

"If something is not done soon, Eliza and the children stand to lose the farm and everything they own," Captain Barton continued. "Your brothers and sisters and your mother and I have all discussed the matter and come up with a plan."

For a brief moment, Clara was angry that she had not been included in the family conversation, but then her curiosity overcame her. "What did you talk about?" she asked.

"We decided that I would buy the farm from Eliza and the three of us—your mother, you, and I—would move onto it. Stephen and David are going to buy this house and farm from me, and Sally is going to stay and keep house for them. Dolly will be here, too, and she will help when she can. What do you think of that?"

Clara was speechless. She had no idea what to think! She was leaving the farm again, but this time her parents were coming with her. She could not imagine what it would be like to leave her brothers and sisters and start over with just her parents.

"Oh," her father went on, "Eliza and the four children are going to stay on the farm as well. The house is enormous, and there is plenty of room for everyone."

Now Clara was even more startled. She was going to live with other children in one big house!

The next day Clara and her parents rode out to visit their new property. The farm consisted of three hundred acres of rolling hills crisscrossed by stony-bottomed creeks that fed into the French River. It was only a few miles from their old house, and Clara had visited it several times before. Now, however, she viewed it as the place where she was going to live. Her father was right: The house was huge. It was three stories high, with a veranda on the first floor and another on the second floor. On the third floor were two large dormer windows jutting out of the roof. Clara hoped that one of the rooms with a dormer window would be hers. It would give her a magnificent view of the farm.

Soon Captain and Mrs. Barton were in deep conversation with Eliza, and Clara found herself face-to-face with her four second cousins. She knew them a little, but she had never played with them. There were two boys around Clara's age and two girls who were much younger.

"Come on, let's play hide-and-seek in the old barn," the oldest boy, Jerry, yelled as he leaped from the veranda rail. "Last one there's a rotten egg!"

Clara, who hated to be the last one at anything, lifted her calico skirt and tore off after Jerry and her other cousin, Otis, who was hard on Jerry's heels. Hide-and-seek turned out to be the perfect game to break the ice. Although they were playing together, Clara spent most of the time alone, hiding behind a hay bale. After they had played for a while, she began to feel a little better about the whole situation. Having boys to play with, ride in the hills with, and hunt rabbits with just might be fun after all.

Two weeks later, the three Bartons moved into the house, and Clara found that her hunch was right. It *was* fun to have children her age around.

She learned a whole new set of skills from her male cousins. She became good at driving a nail into a post and making a square knot that would not slip. There was nothing the boys could do that she could not, or so she thought.

One day, about a year after they moved onto the new farm, Clara's mother announced that Clara was becoming far too much of a tomboy and that she must stop playing with Jerry and Otis and spend more time with the girls. And she definitely must stop pestering her mother to let her ice-skate. That was a particularly unfeminine activity! Clara was furious. She loved being outside, testing herself against nature and the boys' abilities.

Early one January morning, when Clara heard a pebble being thrown against her window, she knew exactly what it was. Jerry and Otis had offered to teach her how to ice-skate while her parents were still asleep. Sunday morning was the only day that her mother did not get up before dawn to do housework. It was the Sabbath day, a day on which the Universalist church that the Bartons attended decreed no work should be done.

Clara felt only mildly guilty as she pulled her petticoat and dress on and crept from her room down the stairs into the kitchen. She grabbed a handful of dried apples for her and the boys to share, lifted her coat from the peg, and opened the back door.

She and her two cousins made their way to a frozen pond on the farm. The boys helped her put on her skates, and then they tied their scarves around her waist. Totteringly Clara made her way out onto the ice. Using their scarves, Jerry and Otis began to tow her along behind them.

The cold morning air turned Clara's cheeks and ears bright red. She laughed and cried out in delight as she glided over the smooth ice behind the boys. Skating was even more exhilarating than she had imagined.

Gradually Jerry and Otis, who were good skaters, began to go faster and faster. Clara squealed a little at the increase in speed, but she did not tell them to slow down. She was having too much fun for that. But as she scooted along behind the boys, her skates hit a patch of rough ice. Suddenly she found herself on her knees skidding across the jagged ice.

Jerry and Otis quickly lifted Clara back onto her feet, but the sharp ridges of ice had slashed her right knee open and severely scraped the other. Blood ran down her leg, and the boys wiped it up with their scarves before tying a scarf tightly around each knee to bandage her wounds. Clara was thankful that her long skirt covered the scarves wrapped around her knees. The three cousins agreed that they would tell no one of the mishap, lest they get into trouble from Clara's mother.

"But you'll have to make sure you don't walk with a limp," Jerry told Clara. "Otherwise your mother will ask questions and find out what happened."

"I won't limp—I promise," Clara replied.

Clara's knees stung, and with the bulky scarves wrapped around them it was not easy to walk naturally, but she did her best. She did so the following day, too, and nobody suspected she had injured her knees ice-skating. However, when she awoke on the third morning, her right leg felt like it was on fire. As she pulled back the bed covers to examine it, she gasped. Her leg was swollen and a horrible blotchy red color, and when she got out of bed and put some weight on it, the pain was excruciating.

She could barely move, let alone walk without a limp. There was nothing else Clara could do but confess to her mother about the ice-skating and the injury to her knees. When Mrs. Barton saw the state of Clara's right leg, she was horrified. It was obvious the leg was badly infected, and she sent immediately for the doctor.

It was the first time the doctor had been called for Clara. Although her leg throbbed, she was fascinated with the instruments in his bag—some of which he used to treat the infection in her leg. Clara chatted away as the doctor cleaned the wound on her knee and then placed a clean white cotton dressing over it. Her knee certainly felt better without a scarf wrapped around it. She, however, was not happy when the doctor told her she would probably have to stay in bed for up to three weeks while her leg healed and the swelling went down.

As she lay in bed recovering, Clara had no idea that she would be seeing a lot of the doctor and even using some of the instruments in his bag in the not too distant future.

What brought her back in contact with the doctor was the result of events that happened on a beautiful spring morning in May 1832. Clara was ten and a half years old by now, and her father had decided to build a new barn on the farm to replace the rickety one built before the Revolutionary War. Because it took a lot of manpower to raise the walls of the new barn and then set the ridgepole in place, the entire community was asked to help. Whole families arrived in their wagons, and while the women and children prepared a huge feast, the men busied themselves hammering the studs together and pushing the walls into place.

Clara loved watching the barn take shape. She listened as her father barked out orders in military fashion, and she watched as her two muscular brothers, shirtsleeves rolled up, shouldered heavy loads.

The most dangerous part of any barn raising was attaching the roof rafters to the ridgepole. Clara's chest puffed with pride as she watched David climb up the wall supports. He was the one chosen to attach the rafters. The rafters were maneuvered into place, and then David, balancing on the ridgepole, nailed them down firmly. All was going well until somehow David lost his balance. Clara watched in horror as her brother tried to regain his balance, flailing his arms about and trying to reposition his feet. But it was too late. Clara let out a squeal as David began to fall feetfirst from nearly thirty feet up.

David's legs seemed to absorb most of the shock of the fall as he hit the ground. He stood motionless for a moment and then crumpled onto the ground like a rag doll. He lay on his back very still as people rushed to him to see whether he was alive. Clara's legs moved in that direction too, though her mind was paralyzed with fear.

Much to everyone's relief, David opened his eyes and sat up. Someone reached out a hand, and David stood up. He wobbled for a minute or two, and then he brushed the sawdust off his pants. "Well, that was the fast way down!" he joked.

Everyone laughed loudly, and several of the men clapped David on the back. Everything was well, or so the barn raisers thought. They continued with their work, and soon the skeleton of the barn was in place. That night Clara joined in the big party, complete with fiddle playing and too much food for them all to eat.

The next day David, who was staying at his parents' farm while the barn was being built, complained of a headache. And the day afterward he was running a high fever and could not see properly. Mrs. Barton ordered him to bed and called the doctor.

Clara was terrified about her brother's condition. She thought it had something to do with the fall two days before, and she told the doctor so. The doctor raised his eyebrows and said, "You know, I think you might be right. Your brother's blood is too vigorous. I am sure some of it needs to be bled off."

The doctor then turned to Mrs. Barton and informed her, "Your son is going to need constant care if there is to be any possibility of his recovering. His condition is grave, and he will need bleeding once a day."

"For how long?" Clara heard her mother ask.

"That I can't say, ma'am," the doctor replied. "But someone is going to have to feed him and bathe him every day."

Clara felt her heart beating in her chest. Her big brother, the brother who was always helping her, now needed someone to help him. She desperately wanted to be that someone.

Chapter 4

Revelations

Clara got her wish. Even though she was only ten years old, her mother agreed that she could be David's nurse. The doctor showed her how to care for her patient. Since the doctor thought David's condition was due to his being too vigorous and having too much blood, most of the treatment consisted of using leeches to suck off the excess blood. Clara watched horrified as the doctor opened a jar of dark, slimy leeches and pulled them out one by one. The leeches had two suckers, one on either end of their bodies. The doctor placed several of the leeches near David's neck. Clara watched as the leeches fastened onto his body with one of the suckers and then burrowed in with the other and began to suck out David's blood. When the leeches were so full they could suck no more blood, they let go and rolled off David onto the bed. The doctor then showed Clara how to scoop them up and drop them back into the jar. By the following morning they would have digested the blood and be ready to suck more.

Clara never did feel comfortable dipping her hand into the jar of leeches and pulling out the slimy creatures, but she learned to steel herself for the task, believing that she was saving her brother's life.

After two weeks David showed no signs of improvement. He could not get out of bed or focus long enough to read. Instead he lay there, sweating and groaning. Clara barely left his side, spooning small amounts of soup into his mouth and mopping his brow with a cold cloth. The doctor came to see David every day, and although he praised Clara's nursing skills, he did not hold out much hope for her patient. But Clara would not give up. She was sure that if she kept nursing David, he would recover.

Her belief was tested by time—a long time. For the next two years, Clara was constantly beside her brother, applying the leeches to bleed him, washing him, feeding him. In spite of all the care, his condition stayed much the same.

The only time Clara left the house was to go to church on Sunday and for an occasional ride on Billy. She wanted it that way. To her nothing was as important as saving David's life, even if it meant sacrificing her own.

Sometimes events reminded her that there was a world outside David's sickroom. There were two family weddings. Her brother Stephen married Elizabeth Rich, and soon after that Sally married Vester Vassall.

By the spring of 1834, the Barton family was looking for some different way to treat David. He could not spend the rest of his life in limbo, lying in pain with Clara at his side. So they consulted another doctor, Dr. McCullum, who believed that a person could not have too much blood and was a follower of a new brand of medicine called "hydrotherapy." This treatment involved the patient's being taken off all other treatments and given regular steam baths instead. Many people considered such advice quackery, but by now the Bartons were so desperate that they put David under Dr. McCullum's care. The doctor came for David in a wagon and took him twenty miles away to a private sanatorium. Clara was distraught to see him leave, but she prayed that the new treatment would make him better.

And it did. Within three weeks of being taken off the leech treatment and having three long steam baths a day, David was standing firmly on his feet and even taking a few steps. He was well on his way to recovery!

Clara was shocked. David had spent three weeks with Dr. McCullum and two years with her. She wondered whether her nursing had helped him to remain sick. Had those horrible, slimy leeches been sucking the life out of her brother? What if she had kept going longer? Would she have eventually killed him? Clara did not know the answers to any of these questions that haunted her.

Now that her job as nurse was over, Clara found she had little to do. She felt even more disconnected from people her age than she had before, and she counted her horse, Billy, as her best friend. However, another person soon needed her help—her grandmother.

Dorothy Barton had lived on a nearby farm until this time, but now she was nearly blind and needed a lot of help. Clara and her mother took turns sitting with Granny Barton. But after looking after David for two years, Clara wanted to be out and about, and nursing her grandmother proved stressful. After several weeks, Clara's cousin Julia came from Maine to help with the nursing duties.

Eighteen-year-old Julia Porter was everything that Clara was not. She was tall and pretty, and being the youngest of twelve children had shaped her into an outgoing and popular young woman. Thankfully, instead of disdaining Clara's shy ways and lack of social skills, Julia took her under her wing and helped her to make new friends.

With Julia in the house, Clara finally began to gain a little confidence in herself—enough, in fact, to ask her father to let her help out in the community. She had discovered how much joy and satisfaction she gained from helping others. This greatly pleased her father, who thought helping others was very important. Besides giving money to the poor people in North Oxford, he had paid for an entire house to be built there for the use of families who found themselves homeless for a time.

Soon Clara was busy tutoring poor children who had trouble learning to read and visiting sick people in town. About this time a smallpox epidemic raged through town, and Clara was soon busier than ever nursing many patients with the dreaded disease. It wasn't long, however, before she herself was a patient, having come down with the disease. Thankfully, she had a mild case, and all she needed was bed rest to make a full recovery.

As she lay in bed, she thought about what she should do next. She was seventeen years old now. Her mother had been married and had a baby by that age, and her sister Sally now had three small children. Was it time for her also to think about marriage? Clara tried to imagine herself with a husband, a house, and small children running around her feet, but she could not. Perhaps it was all the geography she had studied in school, or something else, but she had the feeling that she needed a life different from that.

The thought struck and startled her that she needed adventure! No one would have thought of timid Clara Barton as the type of girl who craved adventure, but deep down she did. A week later she decided she was crazy for thinking she could ever find adventure. It was hard enough to speak to the strangers who passed through town, let alone think of leaving her home. Still, the idea persisted, and a part of her began to wonder where that adventure might lie. There was no easy answer to this question. Young women in America had very few choices about what they could do with their lives, but Clara gave the matter a lot of thought while she lay recovering from smallpox.

By the time she was better, she had made up her mind. She would ask Stephen for a job at the new cloth factory he had built nearby. A job meant money, and money meant opportunities.

At first Stephen laughed at the idea. Two of Clara's cousins already worked at the factory, but that was because they needed the money. Everyone in the Barton family had always assumed that Clara would stay at home helping her mother and grandmother until she married. Besides, Stephen pointed out, Clara was only five feet tall. How would she ever reach the shuttles on the looms?

But she would not be put off. It had taken her a long time to decide what she needed to do next, and she was not going to be dissuaded. Eventually Stephen gave in, and Clara began work at the factory. Stephen even built a platform for his young sister to stand on so that she could reach everything she needed to work on the loom.

The work was hot and noisy, but Clara loved her job and eagerly awaited her first paycheck. However, it was her one and only paycheck. She had been working at the factory for only two weeks when the family was roused in the middle of the night. The factory was on fire! It burned to the ground. Although it was never proved, rumor had it that the fire was arson, the work of a disgruntled creditor of Stephen's.

Whatever the reason for the fire, the result was the same. Clara was out of a job, and she could see no other way out of her situation. She became shy and withdrawn again, and even Julia could not shake her out of it. Later that year her grandmother died, and Clara had even less to do than before. Some days she could hardly be bothered leaving the house.

One winter day Clara came home from church with numb hands; two of her fingers even had chilblains on them. Her mother noticed the raised red areas.

"What is wrong with your hands?" she asked as they were getting out of the gig.

"Nothing," Clara replied.

"Why, Clara, I do believe you have chilblains. You must wear your gloves."

Clara ran into the house and up the stairs. She slammed her bedroom door shut behind her, flung herself onto the bed, and sobbed. *What is the matter with me?* she asked herself. The truth was that she did not have any gloves. She had worn her last pair out and did not have the courage to ask her father or mother for some new ones.

Clara sobbed for a long time, wishing that somehow she could be more like Julia or Sally or just about anyone else she knew. Why was it so hard to ask for even the simplest things for herself when she knew that her father clothed many poor people in town and would gladly buy her the gloves? The question haunted her. Two weeks later she was to discover that it haunted her parents, too.

Once again Clara was back in bed, this time with the mumps. During her illness she spent many hours lying on the daybed in the downstairs sunporch. At the same time, her father had invited a traveler to stay at the house. His name was Lorenzo Fowler, and he was a famous Englishman who believed in a new science called phrenology.

Clara listened silently as Mr. Fowler explained phrenology to her mother in the next room. From what she could gather, it was the science of what went on in the brain. According to Lorenzo Fowler, the brain was divided up into many little compartments that controlled various behaviors, such as cautiousness, hope, destructiveness, and marvelousness. Everyone's brain was different. Some brains had bigger compartments of firmness, and others had smaller compartments of constructiveness. The combination of all compartments made you the type of person you were. By studying the shape of a person's head, it was possible to see how big the various compartments were.

Clara was just about to drift off to sleep when she heard her mother mention her name.

"All of this might be true. I think it probably is, but the question I have is, how can knowing this science help someone like our daughter Clara? She is so timid and shy I don't think she will ever be able to make her own way in the world. Why, she can't even tell us when she needs a new pair of gloves," Clara heard her mother say.

There was a pause, and then Mr. Fowler replied, "Tell me more about your daughter. How old is she? Has she always been so timid? Do you know what made her that way?"

Clara lay in bed, shocked at what her mother was saying to a stranger! Mrs. Barton told the visitor about Clara's reluctance to ask for anything for herself and how she found it very hard to make new friends.

After they had discussed all of Clara's problems for about half an hour, Mr. Fowler made his diagnosis. "I think, ma'am," he began, "that Clara will never assert herself on her own behalf. She will suffer personal wrong before she will ever draw attention to it, but when it comes to other people, she will be as bold as a lion, perfectly fearless. You must encourage her to find a situation where others need her to be outgoing, and I am sure she will rise to the occasion. Clara needs a reason to come out of her shell."

"I think I agree with you," Clara heard her mother say. "But do you have anything specific you could recommend?"

"I think perhaps teaching school would be a good thing for Clara. From what you say, she is very quick, and I believe she will put the needs of the students before her own," Mr. Fowler replied.

Clara lay still for a long time, thinking about the conversation she had just overheard. She wondered whether she would make a good teacher. She imagined herself standing in front of a class filled with students, all looking to her for direction and encouragement. The thought of it scared her terribly, but a little part of her began to wonder whether this might be the start of the adventure she so longed to have.

Chapter 5

Teacher

Clara Barton stretched herself up to her full height of five feet and peered at herself in the mirror. What she saw distressed her. Although she was going on eighteen years old, she still looked about twelve. She had hoped the new green dress with the velvet bodice would make her look more schoolteacher-like, but it did not. Looking at herself made her want to run into her bedroom and cry, but she knew she was too old to do that. Somehow she would have to go through with the plan she and her parents had agreed to.

Up until now all had gone well. She had passed with flying colors her teacher's examination, a question-and-answer session that took place before a judge, a minister, and a justice of the peace. She had been assigned to a summer school in New

Oxford that was to be held in Public School House Number Nine.

Summer school was considered easier to teach than winter school because few boys attended school in summer. Boys were needed on the family farms to tend the crops and harvest them. This left small children and older girls free to go to school, and they were more likely to obey a female teacher.

Even so, Clara could not imagine herself actually standing in front of a class. She practiced her welcome speech until she knew it forward and backward, and then she worried that it would sound rehearsed.

Finally May 14, 1839, arrived. It was to be Clara's first day as Miss Barton, the schoolteacher. With shaky hands and wobbly knees, she climbed the steps to the schoolhouse. She remembered how the previous class in this school had closed early because some of the boys locked their teacher out of the classroom. She felt in her pocket for the spare key, something she determined never to be without.

Strangely, no one was in the school yard, and so Clara pushed open the classroom door. Forty sets of eyes met hers. She froze in terror, unwilling to go forward, unable to go back. It was the longest moment of her life, until she finally willed her legs to walk to the front of the room.

The welcome speech, which she had rehearsed so many times, fled from her mind, and she was left staring at the class. In her panic she reached for the Bible on the teacher's table. It fell open at

Matthew chapter five, and without thinking she began reading the Sermon on the Mount to the children.

As she read, her courage grew, until by the end she was able to look up and survey her students. Just as she expected, they were mainly small children and older girls, though she did notice four teenage boys smirking in the back row.

Once the reading was over, Clara set the children to work reading aloud and spelling. She moved around the room listening to each student, trying to work out how much they knew and what they needed to learn next. She recalled her own experience on the first day of school and took special notice of the smallest children, allowing them to show her what they knew instead of assuming they all belonged in the first grade.

The boys at the back, who were much taller and stronger than Clara, spent much of the morning laughing and fooling around. Clara desperately needed a way to keep their attention and to interest them in study. She was very relieved when lunchtime came and the children all took their lunch pails and sat under the trees in the yard to eat. Clara joined them, though she could hardly eat a thing. She watched as one of the oldest boys produced a bat and ball and proceeded to recruit the other students to play a game of baseball.

As Clara watched them assemble into two teams and start playing, she realized that none of them knew how to put a spin on the ball as they pitched it. It was a technique she had learned years before from David, and she knew she was expert at it. Suddenly she had an idea.

"Here, throw the ball to me," Clara yelled as she stood up.

The boy with the ball looked puzzled for a moment and then threw it. Clara caught it easily and then yelled, "Now watch me. If you twist your wrist like this, you'll get a much faster pitch."

She released the ball, which whizzed through the air. Everyone watched it sail past the catcher and thump against the stone building. One of the boys grinned at Clara. Instinctively she knew she had found her way to relate to the older boys. She joined in the game, hitching up her skirt and running from base to base like the children. In fact, she had so much fun, she almost felt like one of the children herself.

When lunch recess was over, out of breath they all climbed the steps to the classroom, where the students sat quietly while Clara read from a geography book. After that the older boys settled down to work hard for their petite teacher. They hung around after school to carry her books home and copied things for her at the top of the chalkboard, where she could not reach.

Summer school sped by, and Clara continued to join in the lunchtime games. The boys soon realized that if they won against her, it was because she let them. By the end of summer, many of the parents complimented Clara on her excellent discipline. She was puzzled by this and would often reply, "But I have never had to discipline any of them!" And she did not. Through the summer she had earned the respect and admiration of her students, who behaved themselves for her.

In the gap between the end of summer school and the beginning of winter school, Clara faced a new opportunity. Her brother David had fallen in love with their cousin Julia, and they were to be married at Julia's home in Kennebec County, Maine. David insisted that he wanted Clara to be their bridesmaid, but Clara was not so sure. Many of her relatives whom she had never met would be attending the wedding. She hated to think that she might make a fool of herself in front of them all. She worked herself into such a state that she became convinced she would ruin the entire wedding. But David would have none of it, and so the three of them—David, Julia, and Clara—set out on the journey north to Maine.

Clara had never been more than a few miles from home, and soon her curiosity got the better of her. They made their way to the coast, where she was awed by seeing the ocean for the first time. The trio then climbed aboard a boat and headed up the rocky coast to Maine, where they were welcomed by many relatives. Clara tried her best to hide her shyness for her brother's sake, and the wedding went off without a hitch.

Once Clara was safely back in North Oxford, she realized how glad she was to have made the trip. It was a small step but one in the right direction, as it had built up her confidence.

Because of her performance in summer school, Clara was allowed to teach the longer winter term, where once again she engendered the respect of her students.

By the following year, she had a reputation for having the most well-disciplined school in the district. Because of her reputation, she was then placed in the various schools throughout the area that had the roughest students. She managed to conquer every situation, becoming something of a legend.

Clara enjoyed the challenge of getting students to learn, but there was one group of children that did not even come to school. They were the sons and daughters of the mill workers. Many of them were employed at her brothers' many mills, and there was no school within walking distance of where they lived. Clara convinced Stephen to allow her to open a school for these children in an old packing shed. It was hardly a fit place to teach. The room had no windows and became completely dark if the single door was closed, and the roof leaked terribly. Goats and dogs wandered in and out, but she knew it was better than nothing.

Clara visited all the mill families, encouraging them to enroll their children as students. On the first day of school seventy children showed up, and more followed. The youngest students were four years old, and the oldest were twenty-four! Some of them were born in America, but many of them were the children of immigrants from England, Ireland, and France. The students often fought and argued in their neighborhoods, but Clara worked hard to make sure that they left all of their differences at home. In her mind, school was a place to learn to get along with one another. To keep the older students interested, she taught them algebra, philosophy, chemistry, and natural history, as well as reading, writing, and arithmetic. Soon Stephen and David built a new school for Clara and her students, now numbering 125.

In 1842 she took some time off to nurse her sister Dolly in her final illness. Dolly died at home and was buried in a quiet ceremony.

After Dolly's death, life continued for Clara as an endless round of teaching school, helping at the church, and nursing sick townspeople.

Occasionally Clara made time for men who wanted to be her suitor. She liked them all, but no one seemed right for a husband, so she stayed single. One of these suitors was Oliver Williams. Oliver was so upset that Clara would not take him seriously that he left North Oxford and declared he would make his fortune in the California gold rush and return to make her his bride. Clara was horrified to think that Oliver was that serious about her. She tried to tell him that she would not marry him even if he were a millionaire, but he set out for California anyway.

Clara spent more years teaching, until she celebrated her twenty-ninth birthday in 1850. It was then that she realized she needed a change. She had been busy teaching children, but now it was time for her to branch out and learn more herself.

She researched her options and found that Clinton Liberal Institute, the Universalist Church academy in Clinton, New York, was one of the few schools that took women. The school was, however, more than two hundred miles from home, and Clara wondered whether she could spend a whole year that far from familiar surroundings.

Eventually the need to do something new won out, and she sent off her application for a one-year course at the institute. A reply soon came back. Clara had been accepted to begin in February! Her brothers were shocked to learn that she would be leaving North Oxford. They had come to rely on her to keep their company books. But Clara knew that, at least for a while, she needed to get out of the small town where she had spent her entire life.

Plucking up her courage, she made the trip to Clinton alone. The first leg of the journey, a train trip, took twenty-five hours. Then she endured an arduous boat trip up the icy Hudson River before catching another train to Utica and finally to her destination, Clinton.

Clara arrived in Clinton exhausted and depressed. She wondered whether she had made the right decision. For the first time in her life, she was among total strangers. No one recognized her on the street, no one knew her family, and most people had never even heard of North Oxford, Massachusetts. And when she saw how young the other students were, she decided not to tell anyone that she had already been teaching school for a decade. The fact that she was ten years older than most of the others forged a big enough gap without their thinking she knew all about teaching as well.

Slowly Clara began to make friends among the other students. She particularly liked Abby Barker and sixteen-year-old Mary Norton. The three of them often studied together into the night.

During school breaks Clara stayed in Clinton. She had saved up the thirty-five dollars per term for tuition, board, and laundry at Clinton Liberal Institute and did not have much left over for vacations or other frivolities.

One of the few things she enjoyed was horseback riding. Samuel Ramsey, a mathematics professor at neighboring Hamilton College whom Clara had become friendly with, often borrowed a horse for her to ride, and the two of them would gallop all over the New York countryside.

Many things on these rides intrigued Clara. One night, after a long ride, she wrote to her sister Sally's son Bernard about her impressions of New York in comparison to Massachusetts. "What we are accustomed to call rivers become brooks and creeks in New York, and what we call ponds they don't think worth calling at all, but what they call lakes we cannot call for we have nothing like them."

Clara loved to get letters back from Bernard and other members of her family, telling her all the news from home. However, in the first week of July, she opened a letter and read some startling news. The letter from Stephen began:

> Dear Clara, how much I think of you and what your feelings must be when this sad news reaches you. I think of you as far away from connections and acquaintances in a strange country and among strangers and none to comfort and sympathize with you in this stroke of affliction. Yet I trust and hope that you will bear it meekly and with fortitude. Our excellent mother is no more. She died this afternoon at a quarter after five o'clock. Her last end was without a struggle and apparently easy.

Although Clara had known her mother was sick, she was stunned by the news that she was dead. Regrettably, it was too late to go home for the funeral. She knew that her mother would have been buried the day after she died, long before Clara received the letter. There was nothing she could do and no one to whom she could express her grief.

It was a week before Clara emerged from her room. After grieving for her mother, she stayed on at Clinton Liberal Institute to complete her year of study. But as the year progressed, she often found herself in tears, thinking of her mother and the home life she would never return to.

When her year at Clinton was over, Clara did not know what to do next. There were only three occupations open to women: factory work, working as a maid (neither of which appealed to her in the slightest), and her old standby, teaching. But Clara did not want to go back to teaching. It had lost its challenge, and she craved something new.

Not knowing exactly what she wanted, she returned to North Oxford to visit her family. But as she had dreaded, nothing was the same at home without her mother around. Her father, who was now seventy-seven years old, had moved in with David and Julia, and Stephen and Sally were both busy raising their children. Clara simply did not fit in anymore.

On a windy day in March, soon after she arrived home, Clara received a visit from her old suitor, Oliver Williams. Oliver was the talk of the town, a man who had made a fortune in the gold fields and had come home to claim his bride. That bride, however, was supposed to be Clara. She liked Oliver a lot, but she did not want to marry him any more with his fortune than she had before he made it. Oliver was very surprised by this. He tried to convince Clara how much he loved her but to no avail. Clara was firm in her decision not to marry him.

At home Clara had the feeling that everyone in her family was getting along perfectly well without her. She had to face the fact that she had outgrown North Oxford. It was time for her to move on permanently. But where should she go?

Right about that time a letter arrived from Mary Norton, begging Clara to visit her in Hightstown, New Jersey. Unable to come up with a better plan, she set out in the fall, unsure of the path that lay ahead of her.

Chapter 6

Back to the Classroom

Mary Norton and her older brother, Charlie, were at the train station in Hightstown to meet Clara, and everyone in the Norton family gave her a warm welcome. The family immediately involved her in all of its activities, from barn raisings to nut-gathering picnic expeditions and family discussions on worthy books.

Although Clara felt at home in this big, rambunctious farming family, after two weeks she knew she needed to find something useful to do. Mary's father, Richard Norton, came up with a plan. He asked Clara if she would consider teaching school, as the winter term was about to begin and no one had come forward to teach a particularly rough group of boys at nearby Cedarville School.

No one, not even Mary, knew that Clara had already taught school for ten years, and Clara decided not to tell them now. If she did accept the position, she told Mr. Norton, she would accept it on the condition that Mary come along as her assistant. This term was agreed upon, and on the first day of school, Clara and Mary set off together in a horse-drawn sled.

When they arrived at Cedarville School, Clara cast a practiced eye over her new students. The young ones looked scared and eager to please, but the older boys met her smile with a scowl. Quickly she came up with a plan to win them over. She selected the biggest, meanest-looking boy and spoke to him.

"What is your name?" she asked.

"Hart Bodine," the boy mumbled, not even meeting her gaze.

Clara recognized his name right away. She had been told he was the most defiant student in the district, so she got right to the point. "Well, Hart, I have been told that you have the reputation of being a great rogue in this school, but I know that that is in the past. I am sure that you will behave well from now on and set a good example for the younger children."

Clara watched Hart smirk as she continued speaking. "To start things off, why don't you lift down the switches from above the blackboard for me."

Hart obediently reached up and got the switches.

"Follow me outside," Clara commanded.

She tried not to smile at the shocked look on Hart's face. She was sure that he was imagining that this petite teacher was going to try to whip him even before he had done anything wrong.

The two of them stood in the school yard. A row of little faces lined the classroom windows to see what was about to happen. Clara reached over, took one of the switches from Hart's hand, and broke it in two. Then she broke it again and again until it was all in tiny pieces. "Here, you do the next one," she said to Hart.

"But, ma'am," he replied.

Clara placed her small hand on Hart's large, callused one. "We might as well destroy these. I am sure I won't need them. You are one of the biggest boys in the class, and I'm going to depend on you and your friends to help me keep order in the classroom. You can do that for me, can't you?"

Hart tried to speak, but no words came out. Instead he broke the switch into small pieces and obediently followed Clara back into the classroom.

After that, Hart and the other boys turned into perfect young gentlemen.

Clara soon discovered that one reason the boys had behaved so badly in the past was that they were bored. Their previous teacher had taught only spelling, reading, and simple arithmetic. Clara soon set about expanding the lessons, just as she had done in Massachusetts, and the boys quickly became interested in what they were learning.

Clara had done one thing in Massachusetts, however, that she could not do in New Jersey. She could not invite any child she saw to come along to school. Massachusetts had a free, state-funded school system, but New Jersey did not. While the state had laws on its books allowing for free public education, the laws went largely unenforced, mostly because of public apathy. Thus only those children whose parents could afford to pay the two dollars per term fee were allowed to attend class at Cedarville. This disturbed Clara a great deal, and she wished New Jersey would start enforcing its laws regarding free education. But she decided it would be best to keep her thoughts to herself, for now anyway.

The school year went very well for Clara, but she was not happy. At first she had enjoyed being part of the Norton clan, with their never-ending round of social calls and pranks. As the year went on, however, the lack of privacy and the constant barrage of visitors began to get on her nerves. By the end of the year, she knew she had to get away on her own again. But where? She did not want to go home to Massachusetts, and so on a whim she packed up her belongings and took a train to Bordentown, eighteen miles away.

She found herself a boarding house in which to live and spent the next few days exploring the town. Bordentown was a bustling place, with Delaware River traffic, the Camden-Amboy railroad, and the Raritan Canal all passing through it. But although the industries that had sprung up along these transportation routes impressed Clara, the social situation did not. On street corner after street corner, she was confronted with groups of school-age boys smoking tobacco and lazing about. She asked some of them why they were not in school, and she always got the same answer: There was no school for them to go to.

This waste of human potential incensed Clara, who set about doing something to correct it. Her first stop was the *Bordentown Register* office. Over the years she had learned that newspaper reporters not only knew everyone in town but also knew those citizens who would help to support a new cause.

Inside the rather gloomy newspaper office, Clara found Peter Suydam sitting at a desk in the back, busily writing an article for the next edition of the *Register*. Not only was Peter the editor of the paper, but he was a member of the local school board as well. He invited Clara to sit down in a worn, wooden chair beside his desk. When she was finally comfortable, and after some initial small talk, Clara laid out to him the need for a public school in town and her desire to start such a school.

"I am sure it is a splendid idea, Miss Barton," Peter responded, "but these boys on the street you speak of, they are delinquents from bad homes. They do not really want to go to school. And besides—pardon me, miss—you are but a woman. How do you expect to control such boys? They will ruin you. And who would pay your salary? The school board has no money for such things. I am afraid it is a good idea, but it will not work."

"Pardon me, Mr. Suydam," Clara interrupted. "I am not some novice teacher. I have nearly fifteen years' experience in the classroom controlling such boys as you say are impossible for me to control." Peter blushed. "And as to salary, I will offer my services free. All I ask is that the school board provide me with a building in which to hold classes and publicly embrace the project as an example to other communities of what can be done to educate our youth. You provide this, and I will do the rest."

Peter sat silent for a few moments after Clara stopped talking. He looked down and rubbed his fingers over the day-old stubble on his chin. He appeared to her to be deep in thought. Finally he spoke.

"Well, Miss Barton, you are a very determined woman. You have certainly provided sufficient answers to overcome my reservations. I believe, from the passion I have seen in you as you speak of these delinquent boys, that you most likely can do what you claim with them. Therefore I shall propose to the board at our next meeting that we accept your proposal and establish a public school in Bordentown. It won't be easy convincing them, mind you; there is a lot of opposition among the townspeople to starting a public school. Many think the money for such a thing is better spent elsewhere, but I think I can convince them of the merits of your proposal."

Clara was delighted. She thanked Peter very much for listening to her and deciding to support her idea and represent it to the school board.

Sure enough, at the next meeting of the school board, Peter managed to prevail over the objections of some of the members, and the board voted to accept Clara's proposal and establish a new public school in Bordentown. Clara was very pleased with the result.

The school board decided that Clara should use an old brick building on Crosswick Street, only a five-minute walk from the center of town, as her new classroom. And now that she had a classroom and the school board's backing, she asked for all the things she felt were essential to equip a good classroom: maps, chalkboards, and new benches and desks. She got them all.

Next she set about recruiting students. Peter Suydam printed up a number of flyers, which Clara nailed up all over Bordentown. The flyers announced that a free public school would begin in July.

On the first morning of school, as Clara walked into the school yard, her worst fears were realized. The schoolhouse was ready, and she was ready, but there were no students lined up and waiting to be let in. A few curious boys sat on the fence that encompassed the yard, but they did not look eager to go inside.

Clara knew she had to seize the opportunity. She walked over to the boys and said good morning to them. She then pointed to a bird's nest and a number of different insects that fluttered around in the yard. She told the boys the names of the various insects and all the interesting facts about them that she could recall. Slowly she began to capture their interest, and the boys followed her inside the classroom. Hanging on the walls were the new maps of the United States, Europe, and the world. The boys were fascinated by the colorful maps and began asking questions about them. Clara pointed out various oceans and continents and countries on the maps. She told the boys stories of the people who lived there and their strange customs. The boys' interest was captured. After lunch the boys all marched back into the classroom and began asking more questions. And to Clara's relief, they all showed up again the next day.

In fact, more and more boys, many of them with their sisters in tow, arrived at school in the following days. The thing that astounded Clara the most about them all was just how eager they were to learn. They did not even want to stop for recess. The children would gulp down their food at lunchtime and run back into the classroom to do more work! Apparently they'd had all the idleness they wanted before Clara arrived in town.

Along with teaching the basic subjects, Clara tried to teach the children how to think. When Harriet Beecher Stowe's book *Uncle Tom's Cabin* was published, she assigned the older boys to read it. Many of them wept for Uncle Tom and the other black slaves, and the boys had many lively discussions on slavery and how it affected the nation.

More children poured into the school, until it was necessary to open a second classroom above a tailor's shop. A second teacher was hired, and Clara took on the responsibility of overseeing her work as well. But soon two classrooms were not enough, and the list of children waiting to attend school grew to four hundred!

In the fall of 1852, Clara approached the school board about building a new public school. A town meeting was called. By now all doubts about public schools had long since vanished, and everyone was very proud of what was being accomplished in the town. Those attending the meeting voted to raise the large sum of four thousand dollars to build a new school—a school big enough for six hundred students.

Schoolhouse Number 1 was opened with great pomp and ceremony in the fall of 1853. Just about everyone in town showed up to tour the modern, two-story building with eight separate classrooms and well-lit hallways.

After the wonderful opening, however, Clara received a terrible shock. Since she was a woman, and since everyone in town *knew* that a woman could not handle too much responsibility, a man was appointed to run the school, and Clara was given the title of "female assistant." She scarcely knew how to take the news. Until now it had always been her school and her students. She had helped with the planning of the new building and hired all the new teachers. And to make matters worse, the new principal, J. Kirby Burnham, had a very different idea of how to run things. Clara always listened to the students' point of view, but Mr. Burnham ran things like an army, giving orders to the children and expecting them to obey unquestioningly.

Some of the teachers stayed loyal to Clara and did not want a new principal, and soon the adults were all squabbling among themselves as much as the children did. Clara's dream school turned into a bitter struggle. By the beginning of 1854, she was depressed and tired. She could hardly get herself out of bed in the morning and dreaded setting foot in the new school, whose opening she had anticipated with such pleasure. In February she lost her voice completely. She waited for it to return, but it did not, and she had to resign from her position at the school.

In many ways it was a relief for her to be out of such a difficult situation, though she did not have a clue what to do next. She certainly did not want to start another public school. If it proved successful, it also could well be ripped out from under her.

So on a snowy morning, Clara made a decision that would set her life on a startling new course. She decided to move to Washington, D.C., and look for a job there that had nothing to do with teaching. Somehow the capital, with its Library of Congress and bustle of political debate, drew her southward.

Chapter 7

The Gathering Clouds of War

Thirty-two-year-old Clara Barton stared out over the city of Washington. It was hard to believe that this was the capital city of the United States of America. It was so behind the times! There was no running water or sewage system for the city's fifty thousand residents, and while there was a grand plan to the city, the reality left a lot to the imagination. "Parks" on the map were merely overgrown cow pastures, and hardly a street was paved. Interspersed among makeshift houses were some impressive government buildings, including the Library of Congress, where Clara soon began going to read. And for the first time Clara saw slaves working in chain gangs.

At only fifty years old, the city was very young in comparison to most European cities. Clara wondered if the partially completed city seemed strange to foreign visitors.

Clara had planned things carefully, since she had only a limited amount of money. With it she figured she could rent a room in a boarding house, where she could live frugally for several months. After her experience in Bordentown, she took the opportunity to get plenty of rest. She did not feel ready to face the world again right away.

Slowly Clara recovered her voice and her sense of well-being. When she had been in Washington for three months, she was invited to a social afternoon tea, or levee, as it was called. Also present was Colonel Alexander DeWitt, congressman for her district of Massachusetts. Clara recognized him right away. He was an old friend of her father's and had visited their house many times when she was a child. The two Northerners soon struck up a friendship, and Colonel DeWitt introduced Clara to Judge Charles Mason, the head of the Patent Office.

One thing led to another, and much to her surprise, Clara was offered a job working in the Patent Office for Judge Mason. It was a great opportunity, with a generous paycheck of $116 a month and a clean, quiet place to work. She gratefully accepted the job, though she was concerned about how the men in the office would respond to a female worker, especially one who drew the same salary as they did.

Clara soon found out she had been right to be concerned. She was the only permanent woman on staff in the office, and the men did not let her forget that a woman's real place was at home. They blew cigar smoke in her face, jeered at her in the corridors, and even spat in her direction. While such behavior disgusted Clara, she would not give up. She was doing just as good a job as the men were. In time the men grew tired of baiting her and settled down to work beside her. She even became friends with some of them. One of her fellow workers, Joseph Fales, eventually invited her to board at his house with his wife and family. Clara accepted the offer and soon became a good friend of Joseph's fun-loving wife, Almira.

By now Clara was glad she had moved to Washington, D.C. She loved the work at the Patent Office—the job had so many different aspects. Sometimes she had to copy documents or diagrams of things that people wanted to patent. At other times she cataloged the weird array of stuffed animals, seashells, and pressed leaves that had been stored for years in the basement of the Patent Office. She went home tired but happy each day at three o'clock. Over time, three other women joined the staff at the office, though they were all widows who took over their dead husbands' jobs.

On the weekends and in her spare time, she would visit the Senate chamber and find a seat in the gallery. She would listen to the popular politicians of the day, including Sam Houston, Daniel Webster, Charles Sumner, and Henry Clay. Sometimes she would even catch a glimpse of President Franklin Pierce.

Like so many other things in Clara's life up to this point, her job was not to last. In July 1855

Judge Mason retired and returned to Iowa to run his farm. Samuel Shugert, a young man eager to please his boss, Secretary of the Interior Robert McClelland, replaced the judge at the Patent Office. McClelland had never approved of Judge Mason's employing women, and so he ordered Samuel to get rid of them. The problem was that Clara was one of the best workers in the office. Samuel searched for a way to save her job, and eventually a compromise was worked out. Clara was not allowed to work alongside the men anymore, but she could do her work at home. She could still copy legal documents, but instead of receiving a salary, she would be paid ten cents for every hundred words she copied.

It was not an ideal solution, but since there was little she could do about it, she accepted the compromise. Although she now worked harder than ever, with the new scheme she could not make the same amount of money as before. Still, she worked on.

Despite the fact that she had huge calluses on her fingers from holding a pen and copying documents for long periods, she continued to write letters to thirty or more people, including family members and many of her past students. One person she especially looked forward to hearing from was her brother Stephen. Early in 1856 he had persuaded twenty other men from North Oxford to help him found a mill town on the Chowan River in Hertford County, North Carolina. He named the new town Bartonsville. Stephen's son Sam and Sally's younger son, Bernard, had also gone along.

Clara hoped to be able to visit them all and see the growing town for herself one day.

In 1857, the year in which James Buchanan became president, Clara came down with malaria, a common disease in the steamy summer months in Washington. As she lay recovering, she made up her mind to return to North Oxford for Christmas.

Back home she found everything much as she had left it. North Oxford was still a sleepy little northern town. Her father, who was now eighty-three, had become deaf and was living with Clara's brother David and his family in the house in which she had been born.

Clara intended to stay only a short time, but once she had left Washington, D.C., she found she had little enthusiasm for returning to the never-ending document copying. Instead she went to visit her cousin, Judge Ira Barton, in nearby Worcester. Ira persuaded Clara to stay longer, and she enrolled in French and painting classes.

Soon, though, disaster struck the Barton family again. Sally's eighteen-year-old son, Irving, came down with tuberculosis, and Clara rushed to help him. There was little she or anyone could do. The doctor's only recommendation was to take him to Chicago for a "prairie cure." By this he meant that a change of air might help Irving. Neither Sally nor her husband, Vester, was good at handling money, and there was none to spare. So Clara used the last of her savings to escort Sally and Irving to Illinois.

Once there, Clara hardly noticed anything about the state, she was so intent on nursing Irving. With her constant care, his condition began to improve a little. After he had improved enough that Clara felt comfortable leaving her nephew in Sally's care, she returned to Massachusetts to help David and Julia care for her father.

Two years later Clara was still living in North Oxford when she received word that the new commissioner of the Patent Office was offering her a job back in the office. By this time she definitely needed something to focus on, and she gladly accepted the offer. She hurriedly boarded a train for Washington. The train south was particularly crowded, as many people were pouring into the capital at that time. The elections of November 1860 had just taken place, and an unknown lawyer from Illinois had been voted in as the new president. Now people were moving to Washington in the hope of being appointed to political positions in the new administration.

When Clara stepped off the train in Washington, she found the city quite a different place from the city she had left. Washington was in the South, and southern states were angry over stiff, new tariffs proposed on imported manufactured goods and over a plan to ban any new state that joined the Union from practicing slavery. In fact, while Clara had been riding on the train, South Carolina had announced it was seceding from the Union. With the help of militiamen and volunteers, South Carolinians moved in to seize federal property, including military installations. No one knew what this bold move might lead to next, but everyone had a prediction.

Clara believed that it was all a storm in a teacup and that given a little time, the hotheaded Southern politicians would learn to work with the new president and his cabinet. Surely, she wrote to her family, the bonds that bound the United States to each other were too strong to be broken.

Back in Washington, Clara once again boarded with her old friends Almira and Joseph Fales and went back to work at the Patent Office. On February 22, 1861, Abraham Lincoln finally arrived in Washington to be sworn in as president. That day things were very tense. Clara, like everyone else, had heard rumors that President-elect Lincoln would be assassinated before he was inaugurated. This did not happen, however, and on Monday, March 4, the Patent Office was closed so that all its employees could witness the swearing in of the new president.

Clara had a bad cold, but she was determined to attend the event. She bundled herself up in a woolen coat and muff and set out for the Capitol, where the inauguration was to be held. She found about ten thousand people gathered in front of the east portico of the Capitol for the event. She watched as the tall, gangly new president made his way to the podium to make his inaugural speech. The half-finished dome of the Capitol rose above him as he spoke forthrightly and deliberately about the crisis facing the nation. Clara liked what she heard. The new president seemed intent on facing the crisis head-on. Following the inaugural address, Chief Justice Roger Taney stepped forward and administered the oath of office to Abraham Lincoln.

Although Clara, along with all the other Patent Office workers, had been invited to the Inaugural Ball, she decided not to go. Her cold had gotten worse while she was standing in the chilly air watching the inauguration. Besides, Sally and Irving had just arrived in Washington, and Sally was in the process of moving into a small house she had rented. Clara wanted to save her strength so she could help her sister arrange the furniture and nurse Irving.

Six weeks later it began to occur to Clara just what a precarious position she was in. She was a Democrat, and with a new Republican administration in power, she was in danger of losing her job at any time. The last thing she wanted was to go home again. She set about devising a plan to get to know some important political figure who might act as her advocate if it were rumored she might lose her job. The man she chose was Henry Wilson, one of Massachusetts's two senators. She settled on him because she had heard that he was interested in making the Patent Office more efficient. Clara was still far too shy to ask him to watch over her job, but she did think she could prove to him just how valuable she was to the office.

On a blustery afternoon, Clara set off for the Capitol. As she got closer, she spotted Senator Wilson on the steps and hurried to get his attention before he disappeared. When she caught up with him, she introduced herself and launched straight into a speech on how the Patent Office needed more staff and a general reorganization. Much to her relief, the senator was genuinely interested in what she had to say. He even invited her to have coffee with him to discuss her ideas further.

Clara left her meeting with Henry Wilson feeling that she had made a friend and secured her job for a long time to come. And that may well have been the case, except for one thing: The United States was about to split in two. The North and the South were about to go to war against each other.

The Civil War officially began on April 12, 1861, at Fort Sumter, in Charleston Harbor. The Southern Army, now known as the Confederate Army, opened fire on Union forces stationed at the fort. By now six other Southern states had seceded from the Union, and all of them had accepted Mississippi's Jefferson Davis as the president of their new Confederate union. The Confederates had been blockading the tiny island fort since January, but now they thought it was time to take it over and remove the Union soldiers. General Beauregard gave the order to fire on the fort, and suddenly the conflict between the North and South went from a war of words to a war of guns and cannons.

As soon as Clara heard the shocking news, she began to be concerned about the city of Washington, D.C. What made her concerns greater was that five days later the state of Virginia seceded and joined the Confederacy. Now the capital city of the United States was in a precarious position. It was nestled along the eastern side of the Potomac River, while on the western shore lay Virginia, its newest enemy! Surrounding Washington, D.C., to the north was Maryland. So far Maryland, a slave-owning state, had remained loyal to the Union, but many among the state's population were Confederate sympathizers.

Being interested in how the government ran, Clara was well aware that there were only about four hundred marines and another one hundred U.S. Army troops stationed in Washington. She knew that if the Confederates came across the Potomac River, these soldiers would offer scant protection. What was even worse than knowing that the enemy lay just over the river was not knowing how many of them were in their midst. Hundreds, if not thousands, of people in Washington did not like or trust President Lincoln. Some said he was much too northern in his thinking, while others criticized him for being married to Mary Todd Lincoln, a Kentuckian with a brother and three half brothers enlisted in the Confederate army.

It seemed that everyone was being pulled in a different direction, like taffy. Newspapers reported the stories of the commander of the Washington navy shipyard filling bombshells with sawdust instead of explosives and of Lincoln's own gardener selling official papers to the South. In the midst of this confusion, six more states—Mississippi, Florida, Alabama, Georgia, Louisiana, and Texas—seceded from the Union, and President Lincoln sent out a call for seventy-five thousand volunteers to fight for the Union.

People in Washington waited eagerly for some of these troops to arrive. Many feared that the South would invade them before help could get there. But on Saturday, April 20, 1861, Sally rushed in to tell Clara that the Sixth Massachusetts Regiment was expected to arrive in the city by train later that day. Clara was overjoyed. Not only was help coming, but also the regiment was made up of men from Worcester and its surrounding villages, including North Oxford. Clara quickly put on a bonnet and grabbed her shawl. Some of her ex-students would surely be among the men of the regiment, and she intended to give them a hearty welcome.

Clara and Sally made their way to the railway station to meet the men from Massachusetts. They were shocked at what they found when they arrived at the station. The men of the Sixth Massachusetts Regiment were bruised and bloodied. Clara recognized one of the men as an old student of hers and made her way over to him. The young man looked relieved to finally see someone he knew. His bloodied face lit up with a broad smile. "Miss Barton," he exclaimed.

"It is good to see you, James," Clara said, reaching out for his hand. "Tell me, what happened."

"It was in Baltimore, ma'am," the soldier began. "We had to change trains there. We had to walk about a mile to the station to get the next train, and as we made our way through the streets, Southern sympathizers in the city attacked us with clubs. The crowd killed four of us, and the rest of us were bruised and battered. Then, when we got to the next train, we learned that all our baggage had been stolen. All we have left is what we are wearing."

"How outrageous for the people of Baltimore to treat United States soldiers that way," Clara replied. She turned to Sally. "We must help these men."

Sally nodded. With that they rounded up several of the most seriously wounded men and escorted them to Sally's apartment, where Clara dressed their wounds and nursed them.

As night fell, there was even more sobering news. Confederate rioters in Baltimore had now blockaded the railway and taken over the telegraph office. Washington, D.C., was cut off from the North. The Sixth Massachusetts Regiment was the last one to get through. The situation in Baltimore caused panic among many residents of Washington. Many of Clara's friends fled from the capital, while others hastily boarded up their homes and offices. Rumor had it that a famous Texas Ranger named Ben McCulloch was poised on the other side of the Potomac with five hundred men, ready to make a raid on Washington and kidnap Abraham Lincoln and his cabinet and carry them South.

Clara, though, did not have time to panic. She had wounded soldiers to nurse and gathered any supplies she could find to help "her boys," as she referred to the men of the Sixth Massachusetts Regiment, since she knew so many of them.

She worked through the night, and the following morning she hired five men to carry all the supplies she had gathered down Pennsylvania Avenue to the

Senate chamber, where the Sixth Massachusetts Regiment was being housed.

The men were glad to see Clara and receive the supplies she had brought. They were even more delighted when she went to the podium and plunked herself down in the chair reserved for the president of the Senate. She read to the men from a recent edition of the *Worcester Spy* newspaper. The men soaked up the news of home and were particularly intrigued when she read the account of their departure from Worcester.

When Clara had finished reading, she left the podium. As she walked among the homesick, weary men, the words her father had told her since childhood echoed in her head. "Remember, next to heaven, our highest duty is to serve our country and support its laws." Clara vowed there and then to do whatever she could to help the Union cause. *As far as my small efforts can stretch,* she pledged to herself, *these soldiers will never lack a kindly hand or a sister's sympathy.*

Clara had no idea just how much this simple pledge would mean, not only to the men she was visiting but also, in time, to the entire nation and even to the world beyond.

Chapter 8

Something She Could Do to Help

That night, after visiting the men of the Sixth Massachusetts Regiment, Clara sat at her desk with her pen in hand. She dipped the pen in the ink jar and began to write. "Dear fellow citizens of Massachusetts. Much of what I have seen today makes my heart heavy..." She laid down the pen and thought for a moment. How could she possibly explain the chaotic state that Washington was in or the condition of the Sixth Massachusetts Regiment? Still, she knew she had to try. She wrote about the soldiers being robbed of all they owned, how they now had only the clothes they wore, and how many of them were hungry and lonely. Then she came to the point of her letter. "If any of you so desire to contribute to the well-being of these lads, you may send goods directly to me, and I will ensure it gets distributed to whomever you intend it for."

Clara sealed the letter and addressed it to the editor of the *Worcester Spy.* She knew the letter would take several days, if not weeks, to arrive, since it would have to be smuggled through Baltimore. She hoped that a few people would respond and send smoked meats and dried fruit to "her boys," but she was stunned by the generosity one single letter to the editor could inspire.

Two weeks after sending the letter, parcels began piling up at Clara's door—hundreds of them. Some of them had the name of a particular soldier and his regiment on them; others merely carried the words "To any needy soldier." The packages were filled with pies, cakes, bandages, preserves, tobacco, clothes, blankets, and many other things a soldier might need. Clara was delighted. Suddenly here was something she could do to help the Union soldiers. She reduced her hours of work at the Patent Office and threw herself into the new task.

Encouraged at what one letter could produce, Clara wrote other letters to sewing circles, churches, and schools all over Massachusetts, urging people to collect and make items to send to the soldiers. These letters also produced a flood of packages.

Before long Clara's room was so full of parcels and baskets that she had nowhere to sleep. She needed somewhere to store all of the supplies that were flowing in. She rented a long room on the third floor of a building on Seventh Street. She boarded off one corner to live in while using the rest of the space for storage.

Every day Clara went on a scouting trip over the tent-scattered rises around Washington. She took whatever supplies she had with her and kept an eye out for ways in which she could help the soldiers.

By now Clara was convinced that Washington would soon be attacked, and she wrote in her journal, "*If it must be,* let it come, and when there is no longer a soldier's arm to raise the Stars and Stripes above our Capitol, may God give me strength to mine."

After her scouting trips around Washington, Clara would often write to her father and tell him what she had seen that day. In one letter she let him know just how determined she was to do her part:

> I am satisfied that these times will bring out as brave men as ever graced the pages of history, and Massachusetts leads the van.... We trust we are ready to bind the wounds or bear them of our own, if necessary. I shall remain here while anyone remains, and do whatever comes to my hand. I may be compelled to *face* danger, but *never fear it,* and while our soldiers can stand and *fight,* I can stand and feed and nurse them.

Indeed Clara did all she could to prepare for the battles that lay ahead. She visited hospitals. She encouraged people to share what they had with the soldiers. She also wrote letters to everyone she could think of, begging for food and supplies. She had no doubt that very soon the war would erupt in massive bloodshed.

Clara's conviction grew as the hot days of July 1861 went by. Finally, on July 21, thirty-five thousand Union men under the command of General Irwin McDowell attacked a Confederate army of thirty thousand at Bull Run Creek, in Northern Virginia, west of Washington, D.C. Neither army was well disciplined, and the fighting went back and forth throughout the day. Finally the Confederate army, under the urging of Brigadier General Thomas Jackson, had rallied and eventually routed the Union army. The Union soldiers fled the battlefield back to Washington.

As hundreds of wounded soldiers poured back into the city, Armory Square, Judiciary Square, and the large hall at the Patent Office were all converted into makeshift hospitals. Clara sprang into action, supplying food and bedding to the men, comforting them, and writing letters home to their families. But it was so little, and there was so much to do. Clara pressed many of her friends into helping with her work.

When the wounded men were still being brought in five days after the battle, Clara began to realize just how inadequate the care of the wounded was. One man, whom she accompanied to Sally's house for nursing, had been lying in the open battlefield the entire time, and his toes were so infected that they dropped off when Clara moved him.

She wanted to throw up, but she carefully hid her feelings and bathed the man's toeless feet. All the time, though, she was thinking about what could be done about this problem. Wounded men needed and deserved immediate help. Many other women in Washington were doing a job similar to Clara's. Many of these women were part of the U.S. Sanitary Commission, a hastily created government department consisting of thousands of volunteers who gathered supplies, ripped up sheets and towels for bandages, and nursed the wounded in the military hospitals. The Reverend Henry Bellows and Dorothea Dix headed this commission. Other women helped with such groups as Soldiers Aid Societies and the Christian Commission.

Because Clara could see that the wounded were eventually taken care of once they got to the hospitals, she turned her attention to reaching the men as soon after they were wounded as possible. She believed many lives were unnecessarily lost during those crucial minutes, hours, or days. But what could she do? All the doctors and nurses at the front were men, and although she was dimly aware that two or three women had graduated from medical colleges, none of them had jobs that involved nursing men directly after a battle. It simply would not be proper for a woman to do that.

Clara wrestled with how to respond. She wrote in her journal, "I struggled long and hard with my sense of propriety—with the appalling fact that I was only a woman whispering in one ear and thundering in the other, the groans of suffering men dying like dogs, unfed and unsheltered."

While she figured out what to do next, Clara continued visiting soldiers and collecting supplies. Her nephew, Bernard Vassall, was now serving in the DeWitt Guards, which soon became one of the regiments she visited most often.

In February 1862 Clara received a letter saying that her eighty-eight-year-old father was fading fast. She took leave from her job at the Patent Office, turned her warehouse and mailbox over to her friend Almira Fales, and hurried home to see her father one last time. When she arrived, she found that his body was very weak but his brain was still active, and he wanted to talk.

Clara sat by his bedside for hours as he retold the war stories she had known since childhood. Her father wanted to talk about the Civil War, too, and hear all about Clara's involvement with the Union soldiers. On one occasion Clara read a newspaper article to him that recounted the events of March 9, 1862. The Confederate ironclad ship, the CSS *Virginia* (originally the USS *Merrimac*), and the new Union ironclad ship, the USS *Monitor*, had engaged in a pitched battle in the sea of Hampton Roads, Virginia. The battle had been declared a draw, but, the article pointed out, despite the inconclusive result, it signaled a new era in naval warfare.

"Ah, it is a very different war this than those I fought in," Clara's father commented.

"It is, Papa, very different. And not just on the water but on the battlefield, too. The new rifled muskets the soldiers are using are accurate over a long range, not like the old muskets you used when you fought. And with the new minié bullets, they can kill a man from a thousand yards away."

"Yes, the muskets we used were only accurate to one hundred yards," her father said.

"It's a shame that the old generals have not yet properly adjusted for this. They order their men to charge enemy lines as they did in previous wars, and their men are cut to pieces by the new rifles. The carnage is so great," Clara said dejectedly.

"They will learn," her father replied, shakily reaching out and holding his daughter's hand.

"I hope so, Papa—and soon," Clara said.

After several days of pouring her heart out to her father about the war, Clara desperately wanted to go to the front and get to the wounded soldiers as soon as possible. But she was concerned that no respectable woman would be welcome there. As she mused over the situation, her father gave her some advice, which she took to heart. "Hold your head up. Soldiers, even the roughest of them, always respect a woman who deserves it," her father told her. He then reached over to the side of the bed and picked up his most prized possession, a gold Masonic badge. He carefully placed the badge in Clara's hand and said, "I bid you as a patriot to serve your country with all you have, even your life if need be; I bid you as the daughter of a mason to seek and comfort the afflicted everywhere; and I charge you as a Christian to honor God and love mankind."

With tears in her eyes Clara took the badge and pinned it to her collar. As long as the war continued, she vowed, she would wear it to remind her of her father's words.

Captain Stephen Barton grew ever weaker, until, on March 21, Clara knew that his end was near. She and her sister-in-law Julia stood beside his bed as he opened his eyes one last time. He reached out for Clara's and Julia's hands and then closed his eyes and stopped breathing.

After her father's funeral, Clara stayed on in North Oxford long enough to help settle his estate. When that was taken care of, she headed back to Washington, D.C., with one goal in mind—to reach the front lines in the fighting. This was not an easy task, as she was soon to find out. She wrote to the surgeon general, Alfred Hitchcock, asking his permission. He replied with a terse letter informing her, "I do not think at the present time Miss Barton had better undertake to go to the Burnside's Division to act as a nurse."

Hitchcock gave no reason for his decision; he did not have to. Clara knew that being a woman was enough of a reason for most men to deny her access to the front lines. After trying to gain permission from every official or general she could, she had heard all the excuses. "Women run at the first sign of blood." "No woman is strong enough to lift a man's body, so what use would she be?" "A woman might be fine until she recognizes someone she knows; then she'll go to pieces and be a liability to everyone."

Such comments made Clara angry. She knew that she would not run at the sight of blood; she was strong, knowledgeable, and clearheaded in danger. What more could they want? Although many women would have given up their plans long ago in the face of such opposition, Clara was determined to get to the front. She knew that she could save lives there, and that was all that mattered to her.

Finally, in desperation to get to the front, she paid a visit to Major Daniel H. Rucker, Assistant Quartermaster General. She waited patiently in the corner of the busy waiting room at the quartermaster's office in the hope of seeing the major. Finally, early in the afternoon, as Major Rucker surveyed the waiting crowd, all with some request for the quartermaster, many of them trivial, his eyes caught Clara's. He motioned for her to come forward.

Clara walked over, and the major guided her to a seat beside a worn desk on the other side of the rail that divided the desks of the clerks in the quartermaster's office from those waiting to make their demands and requests. She introduced herself before settling onto the seat.

"And what can I do for you, Miss Barton?" the major asked kindly.

Clara opened her mouth to speak, but no words came. Instead, tired and frustrated, she burst into tears.

Major Rucker looked surprised as Clara sobbed.

Finally Clara gathered her composure. "I want to go to the front," she blurted out.

The major looked at her silently for a few moments before he spoke. "The front is no place for a woman. Tell me, why is it that you want to go to the front? Do you have a father or brothers fighting there? If you do, I can tell you that you will not find them by going to the front."

Clara shook her head. "No, I have no family at the front."

"Then why do you want to go?" Major Rucker asked, his patience beginning to wear thin.

"Because I have a warehouse full of goods that I know will be of great help to the wounded at the front."

"What kinds of supplies?" the major inquired.

"Bandages, lotions, salves, and clothes," Clara replied.

"And you have these things stored here in Washington?" Major Rucker asked, his interest aroused.

"Yes. That is why I need wagons to transport them and a pass to get to the front so that I can take them to the men."

"Alright," the major said, holding up his hand. "You have convinced me. The goods you have in your possession are what the army desperately needs." With that the major pulled out several slips of paper and began writing on them. "This slip is a requisition for wagons to transport your goods and for men to load them. And this slip is a pass that will allow you to leave Washington with your supplies and travel to the front," he said, handing the slips of paper to Clara. "God bless you, and I wish you every success, Miss Barton." With that he stood up. Clara thanked him deeply for all he had done for her and left the office, scarcely able to believe that finally she had a pass to travel to the front lines in the fighting.

As Clara made her way back to the warehouse, she thought about how her tears had softened Major Rucker. She thought it ironic that acting like a man, making petitions, writing letters, and appealing to influential friends had all failed to gain her entrance into a man's world, but crying and acting as they expected a woman to act had produced the necessary permits! From now on, she told herself, she would remember that sometimes the odd tear, shed at the right time and in the right direction, might be a better plan of attack than the best logical argument. If men's lives were at stake, she decided she could cry with the best of them.

Now that she had a signed order allowing her passage to get to the front, there was nothing to stop her going. But some things would certainly be a hindrance. One of these things was the hoop skirt she wore. It was fashionable, and no respectable woman would be seen in public without one, but Clara's heart sank when she thought about the situations she might soon find herself in. How could she ride a horse with a man's saddle or squeeze between two wagons with six feet of fabric sticking out around her feet?

As soon as she got home, she took off her skirt and grabbed a pair of scissors and her sewing kit. If she was going to the front, she was going in a simple skirt with no ruffles and no hoop. She was setting a new "nursing at the front" fashion.

The following day six wagons arrived at her warehouse, and Clara supervised their loading. Once everything was safely stowed away in the wagons, Clara, accompanied by two helpers, climbed aboard and set out for Fredericksburg, Virginia. The following day the convoy of wagons arrived at its destination.

The army surgeons eagerly accepted the medical supplies she had with her, and the supplies were soon put to good use. No sooner had the convoy of wagons arrived, than, on August 9, Confederate and Union forces clashed in a vast cornfield in nearby Culpeper County. The Union force was defeated, suffering over two thousand casualties. Soon the wounded soldiers were flooding into the battlefield hospitals, and Clara got her closest look yet at the carnage of war. Wounded soldiers lay everywhere, bleeding and groaning. Some had lost limbs, others had bullets lodged in their bodies, some had broken bones, and still others had open, festering gashes and cuts.

Clara and her two helpers did all they could to make the wounded men as comfortable as possible. They talked to them, cleaned them, encouraged them, and even wrote letters to their families for them. They also set about trying to clean up the hospitals, which were filthy. They also dispensed clothing to the men, many of whom had lost their shirts and jackets in the battle.

In one hospital Clara came upon a group of wounded Confederate soldiers who had been captured in the fighting. Their suffering was as great as that of the Union soldiers, and she knew she had to do something to help them as well. Soon she came back with clothes and what other supplies she had left. With tears in their eyes, the Confederate soldiers thanked Clara for her kindness.

After all the wounded had been attended to, Clara returned to Washington. Her warehouse was all but empty now, and it was time to appeal to people to send more. She took up her pen and began writing letters to her friends and to those who had donated before. One letter she addressed to the women of Hightstown, New Jersey, where she had taught school. In the letter she told how she had carried the goods they had donated to the battlefront and how much use they had been. She wrote, "Your wine brought strength to the fainting; your clothes staunched the blood of the dying...."

As Clara wrote these words, a shudder went through her. Many people were predicting that the war would end soon, but she feared there were many more bloody battles ahead.

Chapter 9

Bull Run

Saturday, August 30, 1862, was particularly hot and sticky. It was midmorning when Clara set out for the hospital at Armory Square. In her bag were combs, clothes, and letters for some of the young men from the Twenty-first Massachusetts Regiment. As she walked, Clara was astonished to see a huge crowd gathered at the Sixth Street wharf. Her heart quickened. That could mean only one thing—news from the front!

Five minutes later she was in the midst of the throng listening to a man standing on a packing crate. "God help the Union," the man cried. "There has been a second battle at Bull Run, and General Pope's army has been routed by General Robert E. Lee's Northern Virginia Army. Thousands of men lie wounded on the battlefield."

The crowd immediately exploded with questions. Which regiments were involved in the fighting? Where was the Confederate army headed next? How many Confederate soldiers had been injured? Clara, though, did not stay to hear the answers to these questions. Her thoughts were on the thousands wounded, some of them no doubt dying that very minute.

She pushed her way back through the crowd. All thoughts of visiting the Armory Square hospital were gone from her mind. She had to get to the battlefield with her supplies as quickly as possible. She half walked and half ran to the houses of her friends, Cornelius Wells, Almira Fales, Lydia Haskell, and Ada Morrell. She told each of them what she had heard about the battle, and they all agreed to go with her to the front the next day.

Next Clara found Major Rucker and asked him for men to load up a railway boxcar that night. The major dispatched ten men right away, and soon Clara and her helpers were frantically supervising the soldiers as they heaved boxes and barrels of supplies onto wagons bound for the railway station. Between loads she wrote a hurried letter to her brother David. She ended it with the words: "I leave immediately for the battlefield, and don't know when I can return. If anything happens to me, you David must come and take all my effects home with you and Julia will know how to dispose of them."

At eight o'clock the following morning, Clara, who had not slept at all that night, stood in the rain staring at the full boxcar, the top of her head barely level with the floor of the car. She heard an ear-splitting whistle as the engine billowed black smoke. There was nowhere else on the train for Clara and the other four to sit but inside the boxcar. Quickly she rolled an empty barrel over to the boxcar door, climbed on top of it, and pulled herself into the car. The others followed. Once inside, she squeezed herself into a spot on top of a pile of boxes. No sooner had she gotten comfortable than the boxcar door slammed shut, plunging everyone into total darkness. The train lurched forward, and Clara steadied herself against the side of the boxcar.

The eight-mile journey to Fairfax Station, Virginia, where the Union wounded from the battlefield were being taken, took two hours. Other trains were also using the line to carry supplies to the frontlines, and the possibility that Confederate spies might blow up one of the bridges while a train crossed made travel treacherous.

Rain was still falling when the train finally came to a halt and the boxcar door was drawn open. It took Clara a moment to adjust to the light. She blinked and squinted as she looked out the door. The sight before her was so overwhelming she could scarcely believe it. Fairfax Station was surrounded by gently rolling hills covered in sun-parched yellow grass with occasional trees scattered across them. It would have been a lovely scene at any other time. Now, bloody, groaning men lay sprawled on the ground around the station in all directions. The only men on their feet were the stretcher bearers taking men from the battlefield two miles away and depositing them wherever they could find space.

For one brief moment Clara felt overwhelmed by the vastness of the task ahead of her. She wanted to turn her head the other way and forget the human misery around her. But then her urge to be useful overcame her initial shock, and she set to work. A soldier placed a ladder against the side of the boxcar, and she climbed to the ground.

The hillside around Fairfax Station was one large, open hospital. From there the wounded men would eventually be transferred to military hospitals in Washington. But for now they lay groaning in agony from their wounds on the hay that had been swiftly spread over the hillside. Amid the human carnage, overwhelmed army surgeons were already busy at work. They wore green sashes across their blue uniforms to mark them as medical personnel, but by now many of the green sashes were stained crimson from blood. Clara watched one surgeon at work nearby. A railway bench had been set up to serve as an operating table. Beside the table was a pile of bloody, mutilated arms and legs the surgeon had just amputated. The wounded soldiers screamed and writhed in pain and shock and often had to be held down while the surgeon operated on them.

Clara turned her attention back to the boxcar and supervised its unloading. When everything had been unloaded, she and her helpers set to work.

Most of the wounded soldiers had not eaten in two days, and so Clara lit a large fire and began to cook a pot of cornmeal over it. She had not anticipated having to feed so many wounded men at once, however, and the supplies she had brought were inadequate for the task. She did not have enough pots and utensils, let alone enough plates and cups to serve the food in. Clara improvised. As the jars and cans of preserves she had brought with her were emptied, the containers were used as serving dishes to feed the men. Never in her experience had a used tin can seemed so precious. Soon, though, the supply of preserves and cornmeal was exhausted, and still so many men had not yet eaten. Once again Clara improvised. She had with her many boxes of crackers and cases of wine. So she crushed the crackers into crumbs and mixed them with wine. To this she added brown sugar, and the concoction was served to the grateful wounded soldiers.

As well as feeding the wounded men, Clara and her helpers cleaned and bandaged their wounds and did whatever else they could to help make the men more comfortable. Among the wounded and dying soldiers, Clara recognized young men who had been her students in the past. These difficult meetings brought home to her in a very personal way the wastefulness of war. She did whatever she could to help these and the other wounded soldiers. After bandaging their wounds, she would sit with them, talk to them, and try to encourage them. She also carried a notebook with her in which she recorded the names of the men who were dying and any last message they might have for their families.

It was taxing, grim work, made even more nerve-wracking by the booms of cannon fire, which seemed to be getting closer and closer as the day wore on. Still Clara forced herself on. She and her associates were the first on the scene to help the wounded men and army surgeons struggling to work under the difficult conditions, and she would not leave until the last man had been safely transported from the field to a hospital in Washington.

A month before, Dr. Jonathan Letterman had been appointed to come up with a system for dealing with the wounded Union soldiers, but he was still holding meetings to work out the details.

Word went out that men were needed to help with the aftermath of the battle and that these volunteers would be paid for their efforts. Regrettably, among those who showed up at Fairfax Station to help were many opportunists. Instead of helping, they ended up drinking more of the wine than they gave out to the wounded soldiers, and they stole supplies. Clara was disgusted by their behavior in the face of such staggering human need.

As the day wore on, wounded soldiers were loaded into boxcars or onto two-wheeled oxcarts for transport back to the hospitals in Washington. It was a slow process. No sooner had one lot of men been sent on their way than more arrived from the battlefield to take their place.

As night fell, Clara did not slow down; the men still needed to have their wounds ministered to.

But with darkness it became difficult to move among the soldiers. They were so closely packed together that it was hard to walk without kicking or standing on some wounded man. In addition those tending the soldiers had only candles for light. Clara was concerned that one of these candles accidentally dropped could set the straw the men were lying on alight, creating an even bigger calamity.

The night was filled with the eerie screams and moans of wounded men. Clara did all she could to make the men comfortable. She pulled socks on their cold feet, placed blankets over them, and, where there were no blankets, piled straw on them to keep them warm.

As she passed one young man, Clara heard him call to her. "Mary, Mary, thank goodness you came," he said.

She looked down at him. In the glow from her candle, she could see that he had been shot through the abdomen and was nearing death. She pulled the blanket over his feet and then sank down beside him to feed him some of her concoction of cracker crumbs, wine, and brown sugar.

"Mary," the young man said again in his delirious state.

It was soon obvious to Clara that he had mistaken her for his sister. Still, she did what she could to comfort him. She pulled his head onto her lap, kissed his forehead, and stroked his hair.

The young man responded by wrapping his arms around her waist. "I'm so glad you came, Mary," he said.

Clara sat with the young man for more than two hours, until he finally fell into a fitful sleep. As she sat, Clara thought about him. He was just one of many thousands of wounded soldiers, yet he was a person somebody loved. Somewhere a mother and father and sister cared deeply for him. She wondered how they would react when they heard what had become of their son and brother. Did they depend on him? Would they be able to cope without him for the rest of their lives? This war between the states was being waged at a high cost to all. One bullet through the abdomen had robbed this young man of following his dreams and robbed his parents of their son and robbed his sister of her brother. Despite the high cost, Clara did not doubt for one moment the importance of what the Union was fighting for.

As the young man drifted off to sleep, Clara decided to do something to honor his sacrifice. Despite his hopeless condition, in the morning she would see that he was loaded onto a train for Washington. At least that way, when he died, he would be buried in the city in a marked grave that his parents could visit. If he were left to die in the field, he would end up in an unmarked grave beside Fairfax Station.

"Miss Barton, there is room on this train only for those with a chance to live. This young man will be dead, if not today, then tomorrow," the surgeon said.

"You are right, sir," Clara replied. "But I have promised myself that he shall have a grave in Washington that his family can visit."

"I admire your sentiment. I wish that could be so for all those who will die here on this hillside. But I cannot afford the space, even for such a noble intent."

"Please, sir, I beg you," Clara said, looking the surgeon directly in the eyes.

Somehow her gaze seemed to soften the surgeon's stance. "Oh, all right, for you this once, Miss Barton," he said.

"Thank you so much, sir. You do not know what this will mean to his family," Clara said graciously.

"Stretcher bearers! Load this man aboard the train," the surgeon ordered.

Once the soldier was aboard the train, Clara made one of the attendants promise that the young man would be taken to Armory Square Hospital in Washington and that his grave would be marked with his name when he died.

Once the train left, Clara went back to tending the wounded men any way she could. And she had more to do now that Lydia Haskell and Ada Morrell had left. They had become fearful for their safety and decided to return to Washington. Clara was now left with two helpers instead of four.

By Monday night Clara was exhausted. Since she had not slept since arriving at the front on Sunday morning, she crawled into the tent that had been pitched for her. However, the tent had been pitched in a slight hollow, and with all the rain that had fallen, there were now two inches of water inside the tent. To make matters worse, one of Clara's helpers was asleep on top of the crates inside the tent, leaving only one place for Clara to lie down and sleep—on the ground in the puddle of water. But she was too tired to care. She lay down and propped her head on her hand to keep it out of the water.

Two hours later she awoke from a deep sleep to the frantic cry of "Miss Barton, Miss Barton, there's been another battle."

Chapter 10

Antietam

Clara was wide awake in an instant. She leaped to her feet, wrung the water from her skirt and hair, and headed back out into the rain. Before long the wounded from the Battle of Chantilly began arriving. Clara soon learned their depressing story. Weary Union soldiers had been retreating along a country road when Confederate General Thomas "Stonewall" Jackson's men ambushed them. The Union men fought hard, but they were outnumbered, and two of their generals, Isaac Stevens and Philip Kearny, were killed in the fighting. It was yet another defeat for the Union, and even Clara was beginning to think the tide might never turn in their favor.

Still, she got to work once again, binding up wounds and the stubs left where arms and legs had just been amputated by tired surgeons. Amputating an arm or a leg was the standard procedure if the bones were shattered and the flesh mutilated. One surgeon told Clara it was better to cut off the limb right away than wait for infection to set in.

Now that the Confederates had won yet another battle, everyone at Fairfax Station knew that they would be advancing on this position. Clara pushed herself to work even harder. Time was short, and if the men were not evacuated soon, the enemy would capture them all. Clara was determined to stay until the last soldier was safely loaded onto a train for Washington.

At about three o'clock that afternoon, a messenger galloped up to Clara. He wheeled his horse to a stop and yelled through the rain, "Miss Barton, can you ride?"

"Yes, sir," she replied.

"But you don't have a lady's saddle. Could you ride with mine?"

Clara thought back to all the times she and David had gone on wild rides through the meadows around North Oxford. "Yes, sir, I can ride with or without a saddle if you have a blanket and girth belt."

The messenger looked amazed. "Well, then, you can risk staying here another hour. I'll be back for you before the Confederates come over the hill, and you will have to come with me then."

This caused Clara to work even faster. She must get all the men onto the train! An hour later, just as the last man was being loaded aboard, the messenger galloped back, holding the reins of a saddleless horse.

"You have to go now!" he exclaimed. "The enemy is breaking over the hills. Try the train. Chances are it will go through, as long as soldiers haven't blown up the bridge a mile down the track. Quickly, climb aboard. I will ride alongside you, and if the train is stopped you will have to jump on this horse and take your chances escaping across country."

"Yes, sir," Clara yelled as she raced for the train. She did not need a ladder to get up into a boxcar now. She had become adept at climbing aboard by jumping from the wheel to the brake-arm.

Clara stood at the door of the car, surveying the scene where over eight thousand wounded Union soldiers had been brought from the second Battle of Bull Run. More than seventeen hundred men were known killed in the fighting, and almost six thousand were listed as missing. The casualty rate was staggering to Clara.

She watched as the conductor lit a torch and set fire to the railway station so that nothing valuable they had left behind would fall into enemy hands. The train began to roll away just as the station burst into a ball of flame and gray-coated Confederate cavalrymen swooped over the hill.

Much to Clara's relief, the railroad bridge was still intact, and the train eventually arrived safely in Washington.

Clara, who had slept for only two hours in the past three days, went straight home to bed. She slept for twenty-four hours, and when she awoke, she went back to work. She had more supplies to collect, politicians to visit, and above all, hundreds of letters to write. Clara took the leather-bound notebook she kept notes in, and starting at the front, she began writing to the parents or sweetheart of every soldier who had given her an address and a message. Some of the letters told of the soldier's injury and where he had been taken to the hospital. But many of the letters carried the last words of dying men. It was harrowing work, but Clara was determined to follow through on every promise she had made.

Clara had just finished this task when an army messenger knocked at her door several days later. When she opened it, he slipped inside, shut the door firmly behind him, and handed her a sealed piece of paper. She ripped it open and read, "Harpers Ferry. Not a moment to be lost."

"Army wagons and supplies are at your service," the messenger said. "And you are to burn this paper now."

Clara nodded and walked over to the potbelly stove in the corner. She struck a match, lit the corner of the page, and dropped the paper inside the stove. She and the messenger watched as the note curled up into a brittle black leaf and then dissolved into a pile of ashes.

"I must go now," the messenger said, satisfied with the note's destruction.

When the messenger had left, Clara stood for a moment thinking through the implications of the note. She guessed that Major Rucker had information that the next big battle of the war was to be at Harpers Ferry, eighty miles away in West Virginia, and that she should be part of the medical team.

Clara, accompanied by Cornelius Wells, set out for Harpers Ferry in a convoy with four wagons containing medical supplies and other helpful goods. They were still rumbling their way across Maryland when news reached them that Confederate General Stonewall Jackson had captured Harpers Ferry and taken thirteen thousand Union soldiers prisoner. Clara also learned that Confederate General Robert E. Lee's army had crossed the Potomac River into Maryland. Despite the fall of Harpers Ferry, Clara knew she could not go home. It was only a matter of time before Lee's Confederate forces clashed with General McClellan's Union army, and Clara intended to be there when the battle started. So her four wagons joined the end of the ten-mile-long military wagon train that was lumbering through western Maryland behind the Union army.

Sometimes Clara rode in one of the wagons, but most of the time she walked alongside. As they made their way toward Sharpsburg, they began to pass bedraggled Union soldiers, their blue uniforms tattered and torn. There had been another battle with many casualties, this time at South Mountain. Clara gave the weary soldiers chunks of bread to eat and tried to encourage them any way she could. She also wondered what she would find when she reached the battlefield. Would it be worse than what she had seen at Fairfax Station in the aftermath of the second Battle of Bull Run?

When the wagon train finally arrived at the battlefield, the sight that met Clara was worse than she had imagined. She took out her notebook and wrote a description of it:

> [The battlefield was] all blood and carnage. Our wagon wheels [are] within six feet of yet unburied dead. A mingled mass of stiffened, blackened men, horses, muskets, bayonets, knapsacks, haversacks, blankets, coats, canteens, broken wheels, and cannon balls which had done this deadly work—the very earth plowed with shot.... It was a fearful way to learn of a battle.... [Cornelius Wells and I are] shocked and sick at heart.

Despite her revulsion at the carnage of the battlefield, Clara sprang into action. She and Cornelius scoured the hillside of South Mountain, caring for the wounded and ensuring that they received proper medical attention. When they had done all that could be done for the casualties of the battle at South Mountain, they rejoined the army wagon train.

As they made their way along, Clara began to think about the order of the wagon train. Her wagons were at the back. Ten miles ahead were the wagons laden with ammunition, next were the food and clothing wagons, and lastly the hospital supplies for the wounded. And worse, the medical supply wagons were often deliberately held back until the battle was well over so that there was no chance of their falling into enemy hands.

To Clara this was a ridiculous situation, since it could take hours or even days for the hospital supplies to reach the wounded men who desperately needed them. But when she tried to do something about the situation and maneuver her four wagons farther up the convoy line, the other wagon drivers blocked her way. There was a set order for an army wagon train, and the drivers were not about to allow a woman to overturn it.

Clara, however, was thoroughly convinced that her wagons belonged right behind the ammunition wagons. As soon as the shooting began, the wounded would need to be attended to.

That night, when the wagons stopped so that horses, mules, and drivers could rest, Clara felt a sense of doom. She was sure that the next day the two armies would meet to fight somewhere along Antietam Creek and many men would be wounded or killed. She had heard rumors that Robert E. Lee had marshaled his Confederate army on the western side of the creek.

Clara slept until about 1 A.M. When she awoke, she had to do something! Quietly she roused her wagon drivers and asked them to hitch up their wagons. They were too surprised to offer much resistance. Then Clara led the four mule-drawn wagons away from the rest of the wagon train through a forest path that came out just behind the ammunition wagons. She fell back in line in the wagon train there and thanked her men.

When the camp stirred at 5 A.M., everyone was startled to find Clara Barton's wagons at the front, behind the ammunition wagons. Clara had won a small victory, which she was sure would become significant in the next day or two.

She was right. At dawn on September 17, 1862, the Confederate and Union armies met each other on the battlefield, and General "Fighting Joe" Hooker ordered the Union army to advance. Clara grabbed her field glasses and climbed a nearby hill to watch the proceedings. Spread across the valley below was Antietam Creek, winding through ripe cornfields. Suddenly the tranquil scene erupted with guns and cannon fire, and soon the smoke from the battlefield was so thick that Clara could not see a single soldier. She hurried down to the wagons to find out what was happening.

"The battlefront is eight miles long, and things are going badly for General Hooker's men!" one of her wagon drivers exclaimed. "He has called for reinforcements, and they are sending in extra cannons to shore him up."

"Quickly, follow the cannons!" Clara exclaimed as she jumped aboard the lead wagon.

As the wagons rolled along, a stream of wounded men limped in the opposite direction, toward their fallback position. Clara offered them bread and water, but she did not stop to help them. Since they could walk, she knew there were many more men ahead who were in far worse condition.

Soon Clara was at the scene of the battle. The main fighting had moved on, and all that remained were hundreds of dead and dying men scattered among the charred cornstalks.

"Where are the surgeons?" she yelled.

A soldier pointed to a small farmhouse to the right. Clara jumped off the wagon, gathered a pile of bandages and a bottle of wine, and ordered the wagon drivers to follow her. Just to the right of her a man lay groaning. Unable to leave him there without doing something, Clara bent down and offered him a drink. She lifted his head with one arm and held the bottle to his lips. Suddenly she felt a pull on her sleeve and the soldier fell back, blood gushing from his chest. His body convulsed, and then he was still.

Clara looked down at her sleeve. It had a hole right through it. Immediately she knew what had happened. A sniper's bullet had gone through her clothing and killed the man in her arms. She closed his eyes, said a brief prayer over him, and hurried on.

She ran through the corn, through a wicker gate, and up the pathway leading to the house. Her friend Dr. Dunn rushed out to meet her. "God has remembered us!" he exclaimed. "We need your supplies; the casualties are enormous. How did you get all the way here from Washington so fast?"

"I followed the cannons," Clara replied, not taking any more time to explain. "Now tell me, what is the situation?"

"There's nothing here," Dr. Dunn said. "All we have are the instruments in our bags and a bottle of chloroform. We have torn up all the sheets, towels, and tablecloths in the house, but they were used up in the first few minutes. There are four operating tables, but with no bandages we are using green corn leaves to stop the blood and dress wounds."

By now the wagons had made their way through the cornstalks, and Cornelius and the wagon drivers began unloading the supplies.

Clara went right to work, cooking soup, giving chloroform or wine to men who were about to have their limbs amputated, and organizing to have the most critically injured men brought into the makeshift surgery or laid in the barn.

By two o'clock the food was all used up, and there were only three cases of wine left. No one had any idea when or if the supply wagons would arrive. Many of the soldiers and the surgeons were very hungry, and Clara hated not having anything to offer them. She ripped open another case of wine and let out a shout of joy. All the crates of wine used so far had been packed in sawdust, but these bottles were packed in cornmeal! At that moment it was more precious to Clara than gold dust. She quickly opened the other two cases and found that they too were packed in cornmeal. Clara set to work immediately making a huge kettle of cornmeal mush.

When the mush was cooked, Clara took it to the barn, which was now functioning as a hospital ward. She enlisted helpers to feed the men, and then she went back to the wagons for lanterns. She had learned her lesson at Fairfax Station: Candles were far too dangerous in a hospital. She had packed a hundred oil lanterns, some of which she brought back to the barn and hung in the rafters and on poles.

All the while the battle continued to rage around them, and stray shells whizzed over the soldiers' heads. The air was filled with acrid smoke and the groans of dying men.

It was getting dark by the time Clara picked her way back to the farmhouse to see how she could help in the makeshift surgery. She found Dr. Dunn sitting at a blood-soaked table, his head in his hands. Beside him burned a single candle.

"Are you tired, Doctor?" Clara asked.

Dr. Dunn lifted his head, and Clara caught a look of disgust and dejection in his eyes.

"Tired!" he burst out. "Yes, I am very tired of this incompetence. Here I am, with fifteen hundred wounded men, five hundred of whom will die before daybreak unless they are operated on, and all we have left is this single candle to work by!"

"Come and look," Clara said, taking the doctor's hand.

Wearily he got up and walked to the door. He gasped when he saw the well-lit barn. "The men are on their way to light the farmhouse, too," she said, "so your work can go on through the night."

Dr. Dunn wiped tears from his eyes. He did not say anything, but Clara did not need words to know how much the lanterns meant to him.

The surgeries continued all night and through the next day and night as well. On the third day the wagons bearing the regular hospital supplies finally arrived on the scene. By then Clara's supplies were totally exhausted. She was glad she had slipped her wagons into the head of the wagon train. Hundreds of soldiers would have died waiting for official army help and supplies to arrive.

At last news came that General McClellan's Union troops had forced the Confederates back to the outskirts of Sharpsburg. The count of dead and injured Union soldiers was tallied, and Clara was shocked at the numbers. Of the 75,300 men who had been in the battle, 2,100 were killed, 9,500 were wounded, and 750 were missing. Rumor had it that the Confederates had lost even more men.

The thought of all those promising young lives being taken was almost too much for Clara to bear.

When she was no longer needed, she returned to Washington, where the air was thick with excitement. The Union had pushed back the Confederates. All General McClellan needed to do now was press the advantage. Surely the war would soon be over!

Chapter 11

Fredericksburg

Fighting was still going on across Northern Virginia, and two weeks later Clara was again called to action. By now she had earned the title "Angel of the Battlefield," and many doors were opened to her. Her friend Major Rucker made sure that she was well supplied with six wagonloads of food, bandages, and medicines, as well as an ambulance cart. Each wagon was drawn by six mules.

Clara introduced herself to the seven mule drivers who would be accompanying her to the front. These men were not soldiers but civilians paid to deliver goods to the battlefront. They scowled when Clara talked to them, and none of them even bothered to remove his hat.

Clara had the distinct feeling there would be trouble ahead, and she was right. They had barely reached the outskirts of Washington when the men began driving their wagons over every pothole in the road. As the wagons bumped along, Clara was afraid that an axle would break, but she said nothing to the drivers. When they reached the Union army post on the banks of the Potomac River, some of the soldiers made snide jokes about men driving a woman into war. The mule drivers responded by telling Clara that they would not take her an inch farther. This made her angry, and she told the men that if they did not have the courage to go forward into battle, they had better quit now, and she would replace them with soldiers. Reluctantly the men loaded the mules and wagons onto ferries, and they crossed the river and continued on their way.

As daylight began to fade, Clara asked the drivers to pull the wagons over so that everyone could get some sleep. The men completely ignored her order and drove the wagons far into the night. Because she knew that they were watching to see what she would do next, she decided to keep calm. Even though the men were stubborn and rude, Clara understood how difficult it must be for them to take orders from a woman.

Finally it was the mules who refused to go any farther, and the seven men had to stop and make camp for the night. While the men fed and watered the animals, Clara pulled the railings off a nearby fence and started a fire. Then she took the tastiest food she had from her supplies and made a delicious meal for the men. When it was ready, she spread a white tablecloth on the ground and called them to supper.

The men ate without a word, but Clara kept up a happy chatter, even throwing in a few of her old New England jokes for good measure. When the meal was over, the men got up, still without saying anything, and prepared their bedding, while Clara hummed as she washed the dishes.

Suddenly she noticed the men coming toward her by the fire. "Come and warm yourselves," she offered, aware that she was a lone, hated woman among seven rough men.

The men stood silently, then one of them, the nastiest driver, a man named George, stepped forward. He took off his hat and wrung it between his hands. "We didn't come to warm ourselves. We're used to the cold," he said, looking at the ground. "We…we came to tell you that we're ashamed of ourselves. The truth is, in the first place we didn't want to come. There's fighting ahead, and we've seen enough of that, and…." He hesitated for a moment and then went on. "We've never seen a wagon train under the charge of a woman before, and we couldn't understand it, and we didn't like it. We thought we'd break it up, and we've been mean and contrary all day and said a good many hard things, and you've treated us like gentlemen. We hadn't the right to expect that supper you gave us—a better meal than we've had in two years. And you've been as polite to us as if we'd been the general and his staff. Well, that makes us ashamed, and we've come to ask your forgiveness. We won't trouble you no more."

Clara reached out her hand to George. "I forgive you," she said. "Your country needs you to bring supplies to the front. Don't stop doing your duty, and I won't stop doing mine. I promise that when you are hungry and without supper, I will be too. If harm befalls you, I will care for you. If you get sick, I will nurse you. I will treat you like gentlemen."

George and the other men nodded, and several of them wiped their eyes. "Now get some sleep," she said. "We need to be on our way at first light."

The men retreated to their blankets, except for George, who insisted that he help Clara into the wagon, arranged her bedding for her, and tied down the canvas flap. Then she heard him douse the campfire and go to sleep a few feet from the wagon. Clara felt confident that she had made seven new friends. And she had. The men never gave her another moment of concern.

There were, however, many other things to be concerned about. President Lincoln was appalled by the high death rate of the engagement at Antietam, and he blamed General McClellan for being too slow and timid to chase the retreating Confederates and strike them a deathblow. Lincoln was so angry that he fired General McClellan and appointed General Ambrose Burnside to replace him. Regrettably, General Burnside was not much better than his predecessor. His strategy was to wait until the Union army had everything in place and then wage full frontal attacks against the enemy.

The news came that a huge confrontation was ahead. General Robert E. Lee's Northern Virginia Army was marshaling on the southern bank of the Rappahannock River near the city of Fredericksburg, while General Burnside's Union army of 120,000 men was gathering on the northern bank.

Clara and the men grew frustrated waiting for the Union army to cross the river and attack. Clara knew that the longer they waited, the more time it gave the Confederates to prepare, but General Burnside would not budge until five pontoon bridges were neatly in place across the river. In the meantime Clara set up a hospital in Lacy House, a large mansion on the banks of the river. She treated men with dysentery, cholera, and typhoid and waited for the inevitable carnage that would soon follow when the battle began.

On December 12, 1862, Clara sat up late. Thinking of what was about to happen made her too sad to sleep. Instead, in the light of the campfire, she wrote a letter to a friend.

> The camp fires blaze with unwanted brightness, the sentry's tread is still but quick—the acres of little shelter tents are dark and still as death, no wonder for as I gazed sorrowfully upon them, I thought I could almost hear the slow flap of the grim messenger's wings as, one by one, he sought and selected his victims for the morning

> sacrifice.... Oh northern mothers, wives and sisters, all unconscious at the hour, would to Heaven that I could bear for you, the concentrated woe which is soon to follow....

When on December 13 the Union army finally crossed the Rappahannock River, 78,000 Confederate soldiers had taken up positions in and around Fredericksburg. Clara busied herself at Lacy House, trying to block out the sounds of Confederate snipers. Soon wounded soldiers began to straggle back across the river.

All morning Clara listened to the crack of rifle fire and the deadly boom of cannons as they belched forth cannonballs with deadly accuracy. The acrid smoke from burning buildings and gunpowder that drifted across the river filled her nostrils with its choking, nauseating smell. Still she worked on, dressing wounds and doing whatever she could to make wounded Union soldiers comfortable. It was already obvious to her that there would be no easy victory here. Judging by the number of wounded she had already seen, if victory came at all, it was going to come at a high cost of Union soldiers.

At lunchtime news arrived that General Burnside had ordered Union forces to attack Marye's Heights, the high ground that rose behind Fredericksburg where General Robert E. Lee's Confederate forces had placed a sizable number of their cannons. As news filtered back to camp, Clara soon learned that this was a suicide mission. In just one hour, three thousand Union soldiers had been killed charging Marye's Heights. From their superior position, the Confederate gunners were mowing down the advancing wall of blue-coated soldiers. Despite the carnage, more and more Union soldiers were ordered to advance on the position. And each advancing line of soldiers had to climb over an ever-growing pile of their dead comrades.

Clara hated to hear of such carnage. She knew that every soldier who fell on the battlefield was someone's son or husband or father or brother. The aftermath of this battle, like so many before it, would be felt in households throughout the North.

Clara was still busy at work caring for the wounded when news arrived by messenger that she was urgently required on the front across the river in Fredericksburg. Another friend of Clara's, an army surgeon named Dr. Cutter, had established a forward field hospital there to treat the wounded from the murderous attack on Marye's Heights. Now, as he was overwhelmed with injured and dying soldiers, he wanted Clara's capable hands at his side assisting him.

To get to Dr. Cutter's position, Clara would have to brave crossing the pontoon bridge that spanned the Rappahannock River and linked her position to the town of Fredericksburg. It was not a great distance across the river—about six hundred feet—but it was six hundred feet where she would be exposed to Confederate snipers and errant cannonballs. Despite the great danger involved in getting to the other side of the river, Clara did not flinch. Her help was desperately needed over there, and if she died trying to make it across, so be it.

Clara took a deep breath and set out running for the pontoon bridge. George, her assistant, accompanied her. As they ran, a cannonball smashed into the river beside the bridge, spraying it with water and causing it to rock precariously. Neither of them slowed down one step.

Clara and George made it safely across the Rappahannock River and soon found Dr. Cutter. Clara rolled up her sleeves and got straight to work. She toiled all afternoon and on through the night. But the following day the Union army was forced to retreat across the river. General Burnside had ordered fourteen charges against Confederate positions, and each charge had been quickly turned back by determined Confederate soldiers. In the end the Union had no choice but to retreat.

The Union loss at the Battle of Fredericksburg was accompanied by an enormous death toll. Nearly thirteen thousand Union soldiers lay dead or dying in and around Fredericksburg. Many bodies were unceremoniously washed down the Rappahannock River.

From its defeat, the Union army retreated to winter quarters, and Clara returned to Washington, D.C., once again sick at heart and unable to put into words the horrors she had witnessed.

Christmas 1862, Clara's forty-first birthday, passed cheerlessly. But in February 1863 she received some startling news. The Senate had appointed her brother David as a quartermaster to be stationed in Port Royal, on the Sea Islands off South Carolina's coast! Clara was anxious to do whatever she could to help him, and she asked the War Department to allow her to accompany David. Permission was granted, and on April 2 Clara boarded an army transport ship bound for South Carolina.

She arrived five days later, having made a very interesting discovery—she was prone to seasickness! The voyage had been one long nightmare for her, and she was very glad to get her feet back on land.

Clara set about helping her brother get used to army life. It was quite a challenge for a fifty-four-year-old man who had never spent a day in the army. Both of them also had to get used to living so far south. The weather, even in April, was hot and humid, and Clara dreaded summer.

Not a lot of military action was going on, because the Union navy was blockading the southern coast. Clara's curiosity was thus turned to the Sea Islands' main population. In September 1862 President Lincoln had issued the Emancipation Proclamation and ordered that it come into effect on January 1, 1863. Now all around were thousands of newly freed black slaves who spoke with strange accents and had little idea of how to live in their new state. Clara was soon introduced to Frances Dana Gage and her daughter Mary, Northerners who had come south to help teach the former slaves how to read and write and make the best of their new opportunities.

Frances was about the same age as Clara, and the two women quickly became close friends. For the first time Clara's eyes were opened to the true horror and aftermath of slavery, and she vowed to help eliminate the dreadful scourge.

Time passed, and although Clara found useful things to do, it was hard for her to justify staying with David when no major battles were being fought around his position. Since she knew that she would be more useful back in the North, on December 31 she said goodbye to her brother and once again set sail on an army transport ship.

Back in Washington, Clara planned to follow the cannons to battle and offer help to the wounded soldiers. But she had another mission as well. The last time she had heard from her other brother, Stephen, he was still in Bartonsville, North Carolina. But that had been well over a year ago, and it was not like him to stop writing. Clara was determined to find out what had happened to him.

Chapter 12

Andersonville

On her return to Washington, Clara began asking various soldiers if they had heard anything of the man who had founded Bartonsville, North Carolina. She learned nothing except that Stephen Barton had sent all of his workers back north to Massachusetts and had refused to go himself because he wanted to protect his property.

Meanwhile, news of Clara's return spread through the capital, and she was soon offered a job. This time it was an official position as superintendent of the Department of Nurses for the Army of the James, the part of the Union army that operated around the James River area of Virginia. Clara accepted the position and was assigned to a deserted plantation called Point of Rocks, near Petersburg, Virginia. General Benjamin Butler gave her passes to go wherever she wanted and order whatever medical supplies she thought necessary.

This suited Clara fine. Once again she was at the battlefront, comforting dying men, making ninety pies at a time to feed famished soldiers, and assisting the army surgeons. She lived in a tiny hut with a dirt floor that only a year or two before had been the home of a slave family.

On the very cold morning of October 14, 1864, Clara was sitting on a coil of rope, supporting a lieutenant who had been shot though the lungs and was awaiting surgery. An orderly rode up and handed her a letter. Her heart raced. She knew it must be important for it to be hand-delivered to her on the battlefield.

Clara wiggled one hand free and ripped the envelope open with her teeth. Two letters fell out. The first was a short note from her nephew Sam, while the other was a much longer letter. She recognized the handwriting immediately. It belonged to her brother Stephen!

With a mixture of fear and relief she began to read. Stephen wrote that he was being held in Norfolk, Virginia, by Union troops. They had overrun Bartonsville and captured Confederate sympathizers. Although Stephen was a Northerner, the Union soldiers believed that he must be a secret supporter of the South or he would have left long ago.

Clara felt her cheeks flush with indignation. Stephen would never help the Confederacy! He stayed in Bartonsville because he was the founder of the town and had a lot of property he wanted to protect.

Soon two orderlies came for the lieutenant she was holding. Clara jumped into the nearest ambulance and directed the driver to take her to General Butler's quarters. When she showed the general the letter, he shook his head. "This is a very delicate matter. What do you want me to do?"

"In the letter Stephen says he is sick," Clara replied. "Could you have him brought to me so that I could look after him?"

"Oh," General Butler sighed, "I suppose that might be possible, as long as you keep very quiet about it. I am putting myself on the line ordering a suspected sympathizer to be freed."

Clara nodded. "You have my word that I will keep him out of sight."

Two nights later Clara opened the door of her hut to find General Butler standing there. With him was a tall, thin man with stringy silver hair, leaning heavily on a cane for support. Clara felt that there was something vaguely familiar about him, though she could not place his face. Then he spoke. A chill ran down her spine; she would know that voice anywhere. This emaciated human being was her brother Stephen. Clara quickly helped him inside and thanked the general for bringing him to her.

Once Stephen was sitting comfortably in Clara's only chair, he told her that he had been in a Union prison for three weeks without the benefit of medical attention or enough food to sustain him. Clara could see that he was very thin, but even she was shocked when he told her that he weighed one hundred thirty pounds, seventy pounds less than when the war had begun.

Stephen wanted to go straight to Washington to petition the government to give him his lands back, but Clara was afraid to let him travel until he was stronger. She set about building up his health with homemade broth.

Stephen set out for Washington before Christmas. In early January 1865 General Butler was relieved of his command, and Clara decided that she would head for Washington to see how Stephen was doing.

Clara found her brother and her nephew Irving at her sister Sally's house. Stephen appeared to be weaker, which Clara put down to the stress of trying to get someone to listen to his land claims. Irving, too, was still sick with tuberculosis.

It would have been a gloomy time for Clara except for one thing. Credible rumors were spreading around Washington that the war was nearly over! The signs were everywhere. The Union blockade of the South meant that many Southerners were now starving. Union General William Tecumseh Sherman and his men were marching through Georgia, leaving a swath of destruction and devastation behind them. President Lincoln's Emancipation Proclamation had set free millions of slaves, many of whom had hurried north to support the Union. Southern soldiers were fleeing the advance of Union General Ulysses S. Grant and his army.

As the war drew to a close, however, Clara realized that many important things would have to go on long after its end. Her nephew Irving had brought one of these things to her attention. Although he was sickly, he had done his best to help the war effort by working at an express office. He had heard that many of the Union soldiers who had been released from Confederate prison camps were in terrible condition. Many of them were in no fit state to make it all the way to their homes, or even to write a letter to say they were still alive. Moreover, thousands of soldiers had been separated from their brothers and fathers who were also fighting in the war, and they had no idea where to meet up. Clara thought about not hearing from Stephen for so long and knew just how it felt not to know whether your relatives were dead or alive.

All of this information invigorated Clara. If she knew one thing, it was that she could organize soldiers. She set straight to work lobbying her old friend Senator Wilson to help her get the permission she needed to go to work on the problem.

Even with the senator's help, the process seemed endless. While Clara waited, she watched Stephen grow weaker, until even she had to admit that he was dying. On March 10, 1865, his end came, and it fell to Clara to accompany his body back to North Oxford so that he could be buried beside their parents.

Two weeks later, she returned to Washington just in time to learn that Irving had died from a hemorrhage, at the age of twenty-six. Clara was heartbroken that neither her brother nor her nephew had lived to see the end of the war. Even the letter signed by President Lincoln hardly cheered her. The letter from the president read, "To the Friends of Missing Persons: Miss Clara Barton has kindly offered to search for the missing prisoners of war. Please address her at Annapolis, giving her name, regiment, and company of any missing prisoner. Signed, A. Lincoln."

Now at least Clara had something to do to take her mind off the two deaths. She planned to set out as soon as possible for Annapolis, Maryland, where the Union soldiers who had been prisoners of war in the South were being processed.

On April 9, before she left for Annapolis, news came that General Lee had surrendered his Confederate troops to General Grant at the Appomattox Courthouse in Virginia. Once Lee and his Confederate Army of Northern Virginia surrendered, the war was basically over. There was no way that the other, smaller branches of the Confederate army could mount any kind of successful counterattack.

The news of the surrender spread like wildfire, and soon everyone was out on the streets of Washington, D.C., waving flags, setting off fireworks, and singing patriotic songs. Clara walked among the crowds, but she could not celebrate with them. The faces of a thousand men flashed before her eyes, and she knew, perhaps more than any other woman in the United States, the shocking cost of victory in the war.

Six days later crowds gathered once again in the streets, but this time they were somber and silent.

President Abraham Lincoln was dead, assassinated at Ford's Theatre by John Wilkes Booth, a famous Southern actor. Now Clara was not the only one who was numb. Everyone was. Even people who did not like Lincoln were appalled at the act. The man who had labored so hard for so many years to preserve the Union and bring reconciliation had lived to enjoy only six days of peace. Later that day Andrew Johnson was sworn in as the new president of the United States.

Even though it was April, the weather was still bitter cold, and Clara quit the mourning city of Washington for Annapolis as soon as she could. The quaint Maryland town, with its circular, tree-lined streets, was overflowing with soldiers. Tents were pitched wherever there was a piece of flat land wide enough for such a purpose. And everywhere around Annapolis chaos reigned as newly released prisoners of war disembarked and were met by crowds of desperate people hoping for a glimpse of a loved one's face. Looking at the gaunt soldiers, Clara doubted that many of them would be recognizable to their relatives anyway.

Some of the men told Clara their stories, which were appalling. The Union soldiers who had been held at Andersonville, in Georgia, appeared to Clara to have had the worst time of all. They had been crowded into a barren, twenty-five-acre stockade that housed up to twenty-five thousand men at a time. The Confederates had provided the Union soldiers with little shelter, and they had sunburned in the summer and frozen in the winter. And as the war progressed, food had become more and more scarce, until the Union men were living on half a cup of rice a day.

More like dying on half a cup of rice, Clara thought as she heard of the terrible treatment meted out to the men. No wonder thirteen thousand Union soldiers had died while imprisoned there.

Even though Clara had the letter of introduction from President Lincoln and an updated version from President Johnson, it took eight weeks for her to find the help she needed to get started. Finally a general loaned her a tent and arranged for all inquiries about missing soldiers to be directed straight to Clara. Before she knew it, she was literally knee-deep in letters. Soldiers brought in mail sacks filled with letters and dumped their contents onto the floor.

Clara quickly started the huge task of opening the letters and cataloging their information. She decided on a simple system for recording this information. When she got the name of a missing soldier, she wrote his name on a list under the state he was from. She planned to publish the list in newspapers, display it in public buildings, and circulate it through national organizations such as the Masons and various churches. This way she hoped that anyone knowing anything about a particular soldier would write to her, and she in turn could write to the person who had made the inquiry.

When Clara called for helpers, her sister Sally and several of her friends from Washington moved up to Annapolis to help, but it was too much work even with a team of helpers. One of the big problems was that the bodies of half the Union soldiers who died on the battlefield or in the prison camps, some 190,000 men, were unidentified and lay in unmarked graves. Clara knew that if she were going to get anywhere with her project, she had to find some way to identify those dead soldiers. But how? There were no records, and many of the soldiers who had witnessed the largest battles were now dead or shell-shocked themselves.

There seemed to be no answer to the dilemma until one day in late June, when a young man appeared at the door of Clara's tent. He introduced himself as Dorence Atwater, a native of Connecticut who had joined the army at the beginning of the war, when he was eighteen years old. Dorence had been captured and had spent nearly two years in Andersonville prison. This information aroused Clara's admiration; not many soldiers survived that long in the army. But it was what he told her next that thrilled her.

"Soon after I got to Andersonville," Dorence said, "I was assigned the task of recording the name, rank, and cause of death of every prisoner who died."

"How I wish we had that list!" Clara exclaimed. "Tell me, how many names do you remember?"

"I can do better than remember them," Dorence replied. "I knew each soldier's death meant something to someone, so late at night, after my work was done, I copied the day's list out. In midsummer it got up to seven hundred deaths a week. Anyway, I sewed the duplicate lists I had made into the lining of my coat."

Tears welled up in Clara's eyes. "Do you mean you still have that list, Mr. Atwater?" she asked.

"I certainly do, with all thirteen thousand men's names on it. And better yet, all the graves were marked with a number, and I have a list that links each soldier to a numbered grave."

Clara rushed over to the soldier and hugged him. It was almost too good to be true, but Dorence produced the list, which was exactly as he had said.

The list of Union soldiers who lay buried in Andersonville was soon circulated. Because it was much too long to be published in regular newspapers, the president gave Clara permission to use the government printing service. Then, on July 8, 1865, Clara found herself among a party of men boarding the USS *Virginia,* bound for Georgia. Secretary of War Edward Stanton had invited her to be part of a team going to Andersonville to mark the graves of the Union soldiers. The party consisted of forty laborers and craftsmen, along with Captain James Moore, the man in charge of battlefield cemeteries, and Dorence Atwater. Clara knew that it would be hard to view the inhuman conditions so many men had died under, but she hoped she could think of some way to help keep their memory alive.

After disembarking, the party set off overland to Andersonville. This leg of the journey was slow and difficult because General Sherman's Union troops had destroyed Georgia's railways and other systems of land transportation as they marched through the state. Clara and the men arrived at Andersonville on July 25 feeling sticky and tired. They were the first official party to enter the compound. Clara thought she had prepared herself for the experience, but still the sight overwhelmed her. She stepped into a treeless stockade with a single stream trickling through it. The stream still stank, since it had been the only toilet facility the languishing soldiers had had to use. Nine acres of trench graves stretched into the distance. Clara turned to the man beside her. "Surely this was not the gate of hell, but hell itself," she commented.

Clara was never one to get depressed at the thought of hard work. Instead, she thrived on it, and soon a proper cemetery began to spring up within Andersonville. Each grave, previously known by just a number, was now marked with a wooden plaque bearing the name, rank, and regiment of the soldier buried there.

To Clara there was something just as sad as the rows of graves at Andersonville, and that was the constant stream of former slaves who walked as far as twenty miles to talk with the woman they had heard was an official from the Union. They desperately wanted to know what President Johnson's new policies toward them were and whether the rumors were true that when President Lincoln died, the Emancipation Proclamation had been overruled. When Clara asked them where they had heard such nonsense, many of them told her that this was what their owners had told them. As a result, many of them were back working on the southern plantations for no wages.

Such a situation incensed Clara. Her years around both black and white soldiers had made her a strong believer in the rights of all men—and women. She hoped and prayed that the situation would soon be cleared up by the government and the freed slaves could enjoy their new freedom.

The Andersonville cemetery was officially dedicated on August 17, 1865. The men had worked hard and finished ahead of schedule, and Clara had the honor of raising the United States flag over the prison grounds. That night she recorded her impressions of the day in her diary.

> Dressing early—Capt. called me to go and run up the stars & stripes—and this at Andersonville! Where sleep those 13,000 martyrs.... I ran it up amid the cheers of the beholders—Up and there it drooped as if in grief and sadness, till at length the sunlight streamed out and its beautiful folds filled—the men struck up the Star Spangled Banner and I covered my eyes and wept.

Now that the work at Andersonville was over, Clara returned to Annapolis and continued with her efforts to locate Union soldiers. Sometimes she thought the job would never end, and indeed the money ran out before she was finished with the project. Determined to find some way to finish her work, Clara took to giving speeches about the war. The speeches raised a great deal of money, some of which she kept for her own needs, and the rest she spent looking for missing men.

While on the speaking circuit, Clara met other women who had emerged as national leaders during the Civil War. They included Susan B. Anthony, Elizabeth Cady Stanton, Lucy Stone, and Mary Livermore. Clara listened to their ideas on women's suffrage and agreed with just about everything they said.

By 1868 the work of locating missing soldiers was nearly over, and dwindling crowds attended Clara's lectures. Finally, too, the strain of all she had gone through began to show. On a cold winter's night Clara walked out on stage, surveyed the crowd, and opened her mouth to speak. But no words came out. Just as in New Jersey years before, her voice was gone.

Clara consulted several doctors and received the same answer. She needed a complete change from the stressful life she had been leading. She could not imagine how she would ever relax in the United States—too many people had come to know and depend on her. As a result, she handed over her records, invested her personal money in the new railroad companies opening up the West, and in August 1869 stepped aboard the ship *Caledonia*, bound for Europe.

Chapter 13

The Red Cross

By October 1869 Clara found herself far from home in Geneva, Switzerland. She was staying with Isaac and Eliza Golay, the parents of one of the soldiers she had treated during the war. Everything was going well, and she had time to take long walks in the fresh mountain air and eat the wonderful, wholesome food Eliza cooked for her. While Clara had no particular plans for the future, two weeks after arriving in Geneva a knock at the door changed her destiny forever.

Standing at the door was a group of Swiss dignitaries. Dr. Louis Appia introduced himself as their leader. Clara was very surprised that they had come to see her, or even that they knew she was in Switzerland.

Dr. Appia, who spoke impeccable English, came straight to the point. "We are all members of the Committee of Five representing the Convention of Geneva," he began, his intense blue eyes boring into Clara's. "Surely you have heard of the Convention of Geneva?"

Clara frowned. "No, I don't think that I have. What is it?"

"In October 1863 a conference was held in Geneva. Sixteen countries sent representatives to discuss the treatment of wounded soldiers on the battlefield. We came up with guiding principles."

"What are they?" Clara asked.

"First, all medical workers, ambulances, and field hospitals should be treated as neutral, and the wounded should be cared for by the first people to find them, regardless of which army they belong to," the doctor said.

Clara's heart beat fast. *How extraordinary it was that this convention existed in Europe when I had been desperately trying to institute similar reforms in the United States,* she thought. *If only I had known about them sooner! Perhaps I could have joined forces with these men and saved many more lives.*

Dr. Appia interrupted her thoughts. "And we did something else as well. We adopted an emblem. Since the convention was held in Switzerland, we simply reversed the Swiss flag, which is a white cross on a red background. We decided to use a red cross on a white background. It appears to have been a good idea because within weeks we were known as the Red Cross movement—an easy name to remember.

"After the meeting each representative went back to his country to bring the matter to the attention of the heads of state. The following year, twelve of those countries returned to sign the world's first international agreement on the conduct of war. Now the number of members is up to thirty-two countries." Dr. Appia stopped and looked into Clara's eyes once again. "We have come to ask you, as an American citizen who has been involved in wars and must surely see the wisdom of such a treaty, why the United States refuses to support it."

Clara was shocked. Was it possible such a treaty had been presented to the American government and they had actually rejected it? She did not think that was possible. "I have been working closely with my government for a number of years, and I have heard nothing of this treaty, or the Red Cross. Are you sure you have spoken to the right people in power?"

Dr. Appia nodded. "Quite certain," he replied. "We have approached the United States government three times and have been turned away each time. I myself have letters rejecting the Red Cross from William Seward, secretary of state during your Civil War."

"Yes, he was," Clara replied. "The new secretary of state is Hamilton Fish. Perhaps he would be more supportive."

"I think not. He, too, has rejected our advances."

"But why?" Clara asked. "I can't understand it."

"From what I can understand, it has to do with the United States not wanting to sign treaties with European powers. But this is not simply a European treaty. We hope it will grow to encompass the world, and we cannot understand why a great and humanitarian nation like America cannot see the benefits of our organization," Dr. Appia said.

"Neither can I!" Clara stated indignantly. She wished she were back in Washington so that she could march right up and ask the secretary of state for herself.

"Why have you come to me?" she asked.

"We have heard that you are very good at publicizing important matters, and when you return to the United States, we would like you to take up the cause of the Red Cross there."

"I think I would like to do that, but I still need to know more about it," Clara said.

"We can help you there," the doctor replied. "I have several books and pamphlets to leave with you. Read them and let us know if you can be of service to us and this great cause we represent."

Dr. Appia reached into his satchel and pulled out several books. "I think you will find this one most interesting," he said, handing it to Clara. "*A Memory of Solferino* is the story of the man who inspired the Red Cross, Jean-Henri Dunant."

Clara took the book and turned it over in her hand.

Eliza Golay insisted the men stay for lunch, and they all continued to talk about the new Red Cross organization.

As soon as they left, Clara retired to her room and began reading the books Dr. Appia had given her. She picked up *A Memory of Solferino* first and was soon absorbed in it. The book told the story of a rich, young Swiss man, Jean-Henri Dunant, who had taken a business trip in 1859. His journey took him through the Italian town of Solferino, where his way was blocked by a battle between Austrian troops and the French under Napoleon III.

Dunant watched from a distance as the troops began to slaughter each other. By the end of the day, over forty thousand men were dead or dying outside the city walls. Although it would have been much less painful for him to ignore the whole battle, Dunant was a compassionate man and felt compelled to do what he could to help. Soon he was organizing food and water for the wounded, setting up makeshift hospitals in churches, and rounding up bandages and ambulance carts.

Dunant returned home to Geneva, but the horror of what he had witnessed haunted him, just as the things Clara had seen at Antietam and Fredericksburg haunted her. He wrote a book about his experiences—the book Clara now held in her hands. He ended it with a challenge: "Would it not be possible in time of peace and quiet, to form relief societies for the purpose of having care given to the wounded in wartime by zealous, devoted and thoroughly qualified people?"

From her conversation with Dr. Appia, Clara knew that the book had been an instant success and that several prominent Swiss men had grasped the vision for such an international organization. One of these men was Gustave Moynier, who had teamed up with Jean-Henri Dunant to call for the first Geneva Convention.

As the months rolled by, Clara remained in Europe, sometimes visiting friends, other times staying alone in hotels, until, on July 18, 1870, war broke out between Germany and France. Within hours of learning of the new war, she discovered that she was going to play a role in it. The grand duchess Louise of Baden, the daughter of Prussian King Wilhelm, paid her a visit. Clara was at the time back in Geneva.

The grand duchess came straight to the point. She explained that she was a patron of the Red Cross and asked Clara if she would organize relief for the battles that would inevitably follow the declaration of war. It would involve her traveling to Basel, Switzerland, where the Red Cross supplies were stored.

As always, Clara jumped at the chance to be useful. Besides, she wanted to see just how this Red Cross organization would do, since the war—the Franco-Prussian War—marked the first time that two countries who had signed the Treaty of Geneva would face each other in battle. She was eager to see whether they could live up to their promises in the heat of the moment.

Clara felt more energized than she had for many months as she packed her bag and headed off to Basel. What she found when she arrived at the Red Cross warehouse thrilled her. She wrote about it in her journal.

> [There is] a larger supply than I had ever seen at any one time, even in readiness for the field at our own sanitary commission rooms in Washington, even in the fourth year of the war.... And trained, authorized, educated nurses stood awaiting their appointment, each with this badge upon the arm or breast, and every box, barrel or package with a broad, bright scarlet cross which rendered it as sacred and safe from molestation.

Since everything was well under control, Clara decided it would be better for her to head for the front. This was no easy matter for two reasons. First, the front was hard to find. As in the Civil War, the battlefront in the Franco-Prussian War continually moved around. And second, the men who ran the Red Cross were not enthusiastic about a woman being on the front lines. Whether she was in the United States or Europe, Clara encountered this same problem.

Eventually Gustave Moynier did agree to let her venture to the front, as long as she took an interpreter with her. He suggested twenty-seven-year-old Antoinette Margot, a French-speaking Swiss volunteer. Antoinette was cheerful and eager to reach the front herself, and she and Clara made a good team.

The two of them left Basel on August 6, 1870, for Mulhouse, near the French border with Germany. However, by the time they arrived, the fighting had moved on, and so they continued north to

Strasbourg, France, where Clara planned to meet with the American consul and get some directions as to where they should go next.

Clara was delighted to discover that she already knew the consul. He was Dr. Felix Petard, a surgeon she had worked with during the Civil War. He seemed genuinely pleased to see Clara and Antoinette, too, and came up with a job for them to do right away. He told them that a group of German-American tourists had been vacationing in France when the war broke out. Suddenly they had become the enemy, and naturally enough they wanted to get to German territory as quickly as possible. The doctor had already hired a horse-drawn bus to take them, but he explained that he would feel much better if someone from the Red Cross accompanied them until they reached safety. He pointed out to Clara that it would also take them closer to the front.

Clara and Antoinette agreed immediately, and the next day they set out for Brumath, Germany. Dr. Petard attached an American flag to the front of the large carriage and rode alongside. All went well until they reached the first German outpost. Clara did not expect any difficulties. After all, they had a busload of Germans on board. The soldiers, however, refused to let them past the checkpoint. Clara watched out the window as Dr. Petard argued with the guard. He did not seem to be getting anywhere.

Suddenly Clara had an idea. If the doctor could not use the German language to convince the guards to let them through, perhaps another, more international symbol was needed. Quickly she untied the red ribbon that held a pendant in place around her neck. She got out the compact sewing kit she always carried with her and used the tiny pair of scissors to cut the ribbon up. She then sewed it onto her white handkerchief and asked Antoinette to tie it around her arm. Clara looked down and smiled. Now she was wearing a Red Cross armband. Determinedly she stepped out of the bus and walked over to the guard.

Before she had even reached him, the guard smiled brightly. "Ah, the Red Cross!" he exclaimed. "Why didn't you tell me you were a Red Cross vehicle? Go on, go on!" He waved with his arms for the bus to travel through the checkpoint.

Clara smiled at Dr. Petard. "Oh, what a wonderful power the Red Cross has," she said.

The doctor nodded as he helped Clara back onto the bus. They arrived safely at their destination, after which Clara tried every way she knew to get to the front lines, but it proved impossible. However, she was soon to prove her worth elsewhere.

On September 30 Clara received an urgent message from the grand duchess. The duchess's husband, the duke of Baden, had captured Strasbourg, but only after inflicting terrible damage. The duchess feared that thousands of people there were dead or wounded, and the survivors were struggling to stay alive. Surely, she said, Clara would know what to do.

Clara and Antoinette set out immediately for the French border town. When they arrived, Clara found the situation to be worse than she had imagined. Barely a building was left standing, making thousands of people homeless. The two women went straight to work setting up kitchens and hospitals and writing letters asking for help.

In the midst of all this destruction, Clara understood that the citizens of Strasbourg had to help themselves as well. It was important for them to feel not like charity cases but like participants. With this in mind, she set up a large sewing room, where several hundred women made clothing for their own and for other families. This served two purposes, which Clara explained in a letter she wrote to a group of Englishmen who had sent money to help.

> My attempts to clothe the people of France have not been the result of a desire to improve the personal appearance...it is to be hoped that few will die of outright hunger during the next six months, but thousands must fall pitiful victims to disease lurking in the only old rags, in which months ago, they escaped from the fire and destruction. Disease is spread from one family to another, until thousands who are well today will rot with smallpox and be devoured by body lice.... Against the progress of these two scourges there is, I believe, no check but the destruction of all infected garments; hence the necessity for something to take their place. Excuse, sir, the plain and ugly

terms which I have employed to express myself; the facts are plain and ugly.

For the first time Clara was helping with the long-term effects of war rather than concentrating on the battlefield. It was a long way from her doctor's orders of resting in Europe, but Clara could not rest as long as she could do something to ease the suffering of others.

Chapter 14

The American National Red Cross Society

On September 30, 1873, four years after arriving in Europe, Clara headed back to the United States. At fifty-one years old, she was not well, mainly because she had done the exact opposite of what her doctors had told her to do. Instead of resting, Clara had once again found a trouble spot and done her best to alleviate the needs she encountered there. But now she was paying the price. To make matters worse, before departing she learned that her sister Sally was dying of cancer. Clara hoped to make it home to see her one last time.

A large crowd of well-wishers was waiting at Pier Fifty-Nine in New York City to welcome Clara home. She rallied herself to greet them all, but her energy soon flagged, and she found she could hardly walk. She suffered from bouts of blindness and often found herself sobbing for no apparent reason. Her family tried to care for her as best they could, but in May 1874, after the death of Sally, Clara checked herself in to a private hospital in Dansville, New York, to rest.

Clara stayed in the sanatorium at Dansville for two years, eating a diet that included large helpings of wheat crackers, raw meat, and citrus fruit. She wandered about the beautiful grounds, wrote chatty letters to old friends, and did a little embroidery. Slowly the horrors of what she had witnessed over the years in the Civil War and the Franco-Prussian War began to subside.

After three years of convalescing, Clara was once again able to look at her future. In the spring of 1877 she read a newspaper article about the developing war between Russia and Turkey. Reading the article stirred so many memories, but this time the memories did not depress her; they energized her. There was a suffering world out there, and she wanted to help! Clara wrote a letter to Dr. Appia in Switzerland, explaining why she had not been in touch with him before now and asking him if she could play a role in establishing the Red Cross in the United States.

Clara waited anxiously for a reply, which arrived remarkably fast, in June. Another letter soon followed, this one from the president of the International Committee of the Red Cross, Gustave Moynier. Moynier welcomed Clara's help and enclosed a letter to President Rutherford B. Hayes asking that the United States recognize the Geneva treaty and allow for the organization of the Red Cross under Clara Barton's leadership.

Clara, feeling stronger than she had in a long time, left immediately for Washington, D.C. She had work to do! She knew it would not be an easy task to persuade the government that they should sign the treaty, and at times she almost wanted to give up. Everyone seemed to have some idea as to why it would not work. The secretary of state told Clara that the United States did not want to be involved with Europe in any treaties. A senator told her that the Civil War had settled the problems between the North and South and there was now no need for such a thing as the Red Cross, since there would be no more fighting.

This last argument against the Red Cross gave Clara an idea. The Red Cross, with its supplies and well-trained staff, could do much more than just offer help on battlefields. The organization could rush to natural disasters and offer those same services to people who had been "attacked by natural disasters."

Not one to go into an argument unprepared, Clara and a journalist she had recruited to the cause spent several days researching natural disasters in the United States. The more she read, the more potential she saw. At least once a year there had been a major disaster in the country. Sometimes it was fire; other times it was a flood, hurricane, or earthquake. Clara and the journalist wrote down the facts they uncovered and marched back to Congress. Clara took her nephew Stephen

Barton with her as well. Stephen was a good businessman and willingly supported Clara's work.

It was hard to find a listening ear, because elections were under way. Clara thus waited to see who the next president would be. James Garfield won the election and was sworn in as president on March 4, 1881. His election pleased Clara because she had spoken to him several times and found him very agreeable to the idea of signing the treaty, as was his secretary of war, Robert Lincoln (Abraham Lincoln's oldest son). With this in mind, Clara went ahead and set up the American National Red Cross Society.

The new society met for the first time in Clara's apartment on I Street in Washington. Not surprisingly, she was elected to be its president. Red Cross chapters soon followed in Dansville, Rochester, and Syracuse, New York.

Sadly, Clara was to live through the assassination of a second president. On July 2, 1881, President Garfield was shot at the Washington, D.C., train station. He lingered for two months before he died. Clara had to begin her lobbying work all over again with the new president, Chester Arthur. During this time of waiting and lobbying, several other organizations had sprung up, including one called the Blue Anchor, that planned to do the same work as the Red Cross, only without any ties to Europe. These groups raised a lot of doubts about the need for the Red Cross, with its international ties, and Clara began to wonder whether the United States would ever sign the Treaty of Geneva.

Clara needed something dramatic to happen to show just how valuable the Red Cross could be, and in mid-September she got the break she was looking for. It came in the form of an enormous fire in northern Michigan. Clara read some of the first reports in from the scene. The reports said that the heat from the fire could be felt seven miles away and that nearly five hundred people were dead and ten times that many homeless. The American Red Cross swung into action, soliciting donations of clothing, food, bedding, and money. Goods and money began to flow in immediately, and the Dansville chapter of the society took charge of distributing what was collected to the needy. Clara stayed in Dansville during this time, and the Red Cross flag was hoisted over the house where she was living. It became both a warehouse and a gathering place for volunteers.

Altogether, sixty-two hundred dollars in cash was raised, and goods totaling at least the same amount were given. Although the Red Cross was only one of a number of groups that helped, Clara quickly returned to Washington to make sure that every member of Congress was well aware of the work the organization was doing.

When the crisis passed, Clara was delighted to learn that President Arthur was in favor of signing the treaty, which he did on March 16, 1882. It was a wonderful day for Clara, as she had almost singlehandedly changed the policy of the United States government. Soon congratulations were flowing in from all over Europe.

Knowing that an average of one serious disaster struck the United States each year, Clara waited anxiously to see what would be the next challenge her tiny organization faced.

The next disaster was not a wildfire but a flood along the Ohio and Mississippi Rivers. It happened in February 1884, and this time Clara hurried to the scene herself. She had never seen a major flood before, and what she saw was every bit as devastating as any warfare she had seen.

When Clara arrived in Cincinnati, the Ohio River was seventy-one feet above flood stage, putting most of the city under water. Worse yet, the water was still rising at a rate of half an inch an hour. Everything imaginable, from dead dogs to walls of houses, raced past in the raging river. Clara watched as policemen in skiffs rescued people from third-floor windows.

Soon after Clara arrived, she learned that Congress had given $500,000 to the area, mainly to find missing people and offer emergency aid. There was no way that the fledgling Red Cross could compete with that type of money, nor did Clara think it should. Instead she saw the Red Cross as helping out the little people in very practical ways.

Clara was shrewd enough to realize that the Red Cross needed lots of publicity if it was to do anything useful at all. With this in mind, she hired a steamer called the *Josh. V. Throop* and invited newspaper reporters to travel on the flooded river with a small band of Red Cross volunteers. A local blacksmith fashioned a large iron cross and painted it red. This was hoisted between the funnels of the steamer, and the Red Cross was ready for action. The plan was simple: Visit the places worst hit by the flood and stay there long enough to find out what the most pressing needs were and then meet them.

During this time thirty-eight-year-old Dr. Julian Hubbell became one of Clara's key assistants. He had first met her while she lived in Dansville and had become very interested in helping the Red Cross to grow.

The *Josh. V. Throop* plied the river, bringing food, clothing, medicine, and wood to make rough shelters to the tiny, isolated patches of high ground. Everywhere she went, Clara also gave out pamphlets on the history of the Red Cross and its mission.

As reports of the work of the Red Cross began to disseminate across the United States, donations of goods and money began to flow in. Six children in Waterford, Pennsylvania, made a donation that came to Clara's attention. They had given a variety show and sent the proceeds, an impressive $51.25, to the Red Cross. Rather than put the donation into the general relief fund, Clara decided to keep it separate and find an especially worthy cause to give it to.

Clara found the cause in a widow, Mrs. Plew, who had lost her husband and her home to the floodwaters. Mrs. Plew and her six young children were huddled together in a hut made of cornhusks near Shawneetown, Illinois. When Clara talked with Mrs. Plew, she knew she had found the right place to give the children's hard-earned money. Newspaper reporters on board the steamer wrote about the touching exchange and the grateful children. Naturally, this story touched the hearts of many Americans, and more money began to pour in. For once Clara actually found she had enough money to meet the needs around her.

When the floodwaters finally receded and the donations were counted, they totaled over $175,000 in private donations. Clara was thrilled at how the public had rallied. She had learned some valuable fundraising techniques that would be useful in the future. People, she realized, needed to have a personal face put on the disaster. When they saw how the lives of innocent victims were impacted by it, they were more likely to give.

In June 1884 Clara returned to Washington, exhausted from over eight thousand miles of river travel. She had barely finished writing letters to thank all the donors when news of a new challenge arrived.

Secretary of State Fredrick Frelinghuysen had nominated Clara to be the first full representative of the United States to the Third International Conference in Geneva. At first Clara did not know if she had the energy to attend, but she knew it was a tremendous honor she could not turn down. Her appointment marked the first time that a woman had been appointed as a diplomatic representative of the United States.

The conference began on September 1, 1884, with eighty-five delegates from twenty-two countries.

Not only was Clara the only American woman present, she was the only woman in the entire conference. From the moment she arrived, she was glad to have made the effort to come. There was so much information available and so many new ideas to consider. She watched demonstrations of portable field hospitals and how the new wonder, electric light, could help light a battlefield through the night so that the work of locating and removing the wounded did not have to wait until daybreak.

Not surprisingly, Clara had something to add to the proceedings. She and another American representative, Judge Sheldon, described their work during the Ohio and Mississippi floods. After the presentation, many European delegates began to wonder whether their chapters should be thinking about doing relief work as well. Clara pressed the point, and the conference voted to adopt the principle of Red Cross action in peace as well as war. This addition to the Geneva treaty became known as the "American Amendment."

When she returned to the United States, Clara took on the task of publicizing the Red Cross even more than she had already done. She traveled all the way to the West Coast, giving lectures, handing out pamphlets, and recruiting new members. Everywhere she went, she explained the work of the Red Cross as "increasing the amount of charitable work done, to systemize what we have, and bring some order out of our past chaos of irresponsible, unorganized, and unsystemized work in that direction." As Clara publicized the work of the Red Cross, the organization grew rapidly, with many new chapters starting in cities across the country.

In 1887 Clara journeyed to Europe once again, for the Fourth International Red Cross Convention. She reported on the progress of the American Red Cross, but she knew there was still a lot of work ahead to make it a truly national organization.

When she arrived back in Washington in March 1888, Clara was stricken with the news that her only remaining sibling, her eighty-year-old brother, David, had committed suicide. It was a terrible blow, and it reminded Clara of her sister Dorothy's battle with mental illness and her own tendency to plunge into long, debilitating depressions.

Even the latest national crisis, centered in Jacksonville, Florida, did little to lift Clara's flagging spirits. This time the crisis was an epidemic of deadly yellow fever. Things went well at first. The New Orleans chapter of the Red Cross agreed to take on the project, and soon it dispatched thirty nurses, both male and female and black and white, to the scene. Clara was proud that the new society crossed both racial and gender lines.

Some of the nurses sent to Jacksonville acted with extreme bravery. Ten of them were assigned to the small town of MacClenny, thirty-five miles from Jacksonville, but the town was under quarantine and the train would not stop there. Undeterred, the nurses gathered their kits and leaped from the moving train as it passed through town. They then set straight to work. They worked for seventy-two hours before stopping to take a break to eat and sleep. Regrettably, some of the other nurses did not take their responsibility to the Red Cross seriously and became involved in drinking scandals. Some even stole the medicinal alcohol from their patients!

Clara was furious when she read headlines like "Drunken Red Cross Nurses Exposed." This was not the kind of publicity the new organization needed.

Slowly, the fuss subsided, but the next time a new disaster struck, Clara decided that she was going to take no chances. She would supervise the work herself.

Chapter 15

Words Fail

It was a sunny morning, the first day of June 1889. Clara was busy tending the patch of flowers and herbs at her back door when one of her assistants burst into the yard.

"Have you heard the news?" he gasped.

"What news?" Clara inquired, standing up and wiping her hands.

"It's Johnstown, completely flooded."

"Oh, that news," Clara said with relief. "Yes, of course. The flooding is much worse than usual, but the Pennsylvania Red Cross is aiding the victims."

"No, no! It's not that at all! You don't understand. This is not about the old flooding. This morning a dam burst ten miles upstream from Johnstown, and they are saying that a thirty-foot-tall wall of water swept through the town, drowning three thousand people," her assistant exclaimed.

Clara's heart sank. "Surely not. The number must be inflated. Come with me, and we will go to the newspaper office. I have a friend there, and he will let me read the messages off the wire for myself."

Half an hour later, Clara stood reading the telegrams, which painted a horrific picture of destruction and confusion. She found it hard to believe that the senders of the messages were not exaggerating. Yet it was clear that many people had lost their lives or their homes and businesses. Clara set the wheels of the American Red Cross in motion.

Five days later she was aboard the first train to Johnstown. It had taken that long to clear and repair the tracks. As the train neared its destination, Clara stared out the window in shock. The reports had not been exaggerated. If anything, they did not convey the full horror of the scene.

Dead bodies and bloated animal carcasses entangled with chairs, wires, wagons, and beds were piled up in mounds on each side of the tracks. And everything was covered with dark brown mud.

When the train stopped at the station, Clara quickly got out and supervised the unloading of the supplies she had brought with her. Dazed, half-naked people wandered around the station. Some begged for food. Others just shuffled past, mumbling to themselves. It was like living a nightmare.

When the goods were all unloaded, Clara looked around for somewhere to settle herself. Few buildings were left standing. Mostly there were just pilings and the occasional walls that stuck out of the ground at bizarre angles. She spotted a railway boxcar to her left. Somehow it had stayed near the tracks in the face of the torrent of water. Clara decided to make that her temporary home. Once her supplies had been stored in it, she set out to see more of the damage for herself. Mostly she walked in silence in the drizzling rain. Because it was impossible to see where the roads had been, she picked her way over the stinking piles of debris. The town was now under martial law, and Clara kept an eye out for some official-looking person.

After an hour of navigating her way through the mess, Clara spotted an officer of the Pennsylvania militia and made her way over to where he stood. His name was General Hastings. Much to her dismay, she soon found out that he had not heard of the Red Cross and had no intention of sharing his authority with a sixty-seven-year-old woman.

General Hastings did, however, give Clara a better idea of the scope of the disaster. When the dam on the Conemaugh River had burst, between three thousand and four thousand people had been washed away. It was impossible to tell for sure, he told Clara, because whole communities were gone, along with most of the businessmen in the town and all civil records. He also told her that they were having trouble with groups of people coming into town and stripping the dead bodies of jewelry and clothing, making it even more difficult to identify them.

Clara was aghast, but she could not convince the general to allow her to help him. Undeterred, she set out for her boxcar. No one could stop her offering help to individuals, and that was what the

Red Cross did best. In the train station she found a large tea chest and dragged it back to the boxcar to serve as a desk. She then set to work.

Everything Clara needed to do seemed to take forever. The telegrams she needed to have sent out took a day to send because of the huge backlog of friends and relatives clogging the lines as they desperately inquired after loved ones. Undertakers from around the state arrived on the second train into Johnstown, but upon their arrival they squabbled over how best to deal with the crisis. Their solution to the disagreement was to promptly go on strike.

At times during her first day in Johnstown, Clara felt alone and overwhelmed, but the feeling did not last. Within twenty-four hours more trains were delivering baskets and boxes of goods addressed simply to the "Red Cross Workers, Johnstown." The American public was once again rising to the challenge.

Tears streamed down Clara's cheeks as she welcomed fifty Red Cross medical workers from Philadelphia. The workers brought their own tents with them, and after clearing some land, they set up a Red Cross village. Clara moved into one of the tents, and the work began in earnest. The largest tent became a warehouse from which food and clothing were distributed. She also gathered together some local women and formed them into a committee to canvass the town, interviewing people and recording their most urgent needs.

On June 10 several boxcar loads of dressed pinewood boards arrived, a gift from the lumber workers of Illinois and Iowa. Some men of the town organized into a building team and quickly constructed a more permanent warehouse.

During this time, two of Clara's best helpers were the Tittles. This middle-aged couple had barely survived the flood themselves. When the wall of water hit, they were washed out of their kitchen window and soon found themselves floating along, with their house underneath them. John Tittle was on one side of the roof and his wife on the other. They clasped hands over the ridgepole and did not let go of each other for several hours. Eventually their house bumped into a bridge and became wedged there. The couple climbed down from the house roof and onto the bridge, glad to be alive.

As more accurate numbers came in, Clara found that many other families had not been as fortunate as the Tittles. In fact, nearly one hundred families in the town had lost four or more family members in the flooding. No wonder, she told herself, that so many people continued to pick and poke mindlessly through the debris, hoping to find the bodies of missing family members.

The new Red Cross buildings got the attention of General Hastings, since he was in real need of lumber himself. The general visited Clara, who offered to share the wood with him. From then on, the general did what he could to help the Red Cross do its work.

The Red Cross used the remainder of the timber and several more boxcar loads that arrived to build three large hostels to house the homeless. It was slow work creating order out of chaos, but in October, Clara felt that her work had been done. She and her team had distributed nearly half a million dollars in money and materials to the people of Johnstown. Schools were reopened, shops were busy, and church bells were once again ringing.

Of course, Red Cross workers were not the only people helping the flood victims, but they did manage to earn a special place in the local people's hearts. The women of Johnstown presented Clara with a medal made of gold and platinum and encrusted with diamonds and sapphires. The *Johnstown Daily Tribune*, which was up and running again, tried to put the town's gratitude into words. The paper said of Clara, "Hunt the dictionaries of all languages through and you will not find the signs to express our appreciation of her and her work. Try to describe the sunshine, try to describe the starlight. Words fail."

Clara was amazed to find that the rest of America valued her work. When she stepped off the train back in Washington, a cheering throng of people was there to meet her. A large banquet was held in her honor at Willard's Hotel, and President Harrison sent a beautiful bouquet of roses to decorate Clara's table. More accolades followed. In November 1890 she was a special guest at a celebration to mark the admittance of the first woman to Johns Hopkins Medical School in Baltimore.

Another exciting thing was happening. Clara decided to build herself a house that could be used as Red Cross headquarters and as a warehouse.

She chose a site in a new development in Maryland near the Chesapeake and Ohio Canal. The house went up fast, and Clara named it Glen Echo. In fact, she was so eager to move into the new dwelling that she did not wait for it to be completed. She was used to living with leaking roofs and doorless rooms, so used to it, in fact, that she forgot that it was a strange way for a Northern lady to live. She invited her delicate niece, Lizzie, to visit her. Lizzie was shocked at Clara's crude living conditions. It caused quite a problem in the family, and Clara apologized for not noticing just how rough her house was.

Three months later, in the fall of 1891, Clara faced a new challenge. This time it was a widespread famine in Russia. The grain harvest had been poor for several years, but in 1891 it failed completely. It was estimated that without some intervention, thirty-five million people would starve to death. Russian Count Leo Tolstoy was asking the world to help. But such a request posed serious questions for the American government. Should the United States give aid to a country whose government repressed its people? Indeed, should one country ever give aid to another? President Benjamin Harrison and the Congress decided no to both questions. They would not give aid to Russia. As a result of this decision, many relief agencies sprang up to try to meet the need. However, they soon realized that they had no way to guarantee that the food would be given free of charge to the people who needed it the most.

Here the Geneva treaty showed its true worth. Russia had signed the treaty and had a small but dedicated Red Cross of its own. Clara announced that the American Red Cross would work with the Russian Red Cross to make sure things went as planned. This assurance helped soothe the confidence of the American people that the food would get into the right hands, and soon western farmers were loading sacks of corn onto railcars. The railroad companies provided free transportation of the grain to Washington, and easterners gave money to pay for the corn to be shipped to Russia. The whole scheme worked well, and the corn from Iowa and other midwestern states fed 700,000 starving Russians for a month. This was only a small fraction of those who needed to be fed, but Clara was satisfied that it was a good beginning, linking people of the world through the work of the Red Cross. She told those she met that she was growing an oak tree of an organization, and everyone knew that oak trees grew slowly but were very sturdy.

Meanwhile Clara did what she could to keep the Red Cross in the public eye, and she had some fun doing it. She attended presidential balls and danced until late. She met with the princess of Hawaii and attended Susan B. Anthony's seventieth birthday party. And Clara glittered in a jeweled dress as she welcomed over two thousand guests to a special banquet honoring the Survivors of the Union Army held at Glen Echo. One of the features of her new house was a reception room large enough to hold the entire group!

On one occasion Clara was invited to speak to the Women's Relief Corps. Just hours before she was to give her speech, she decided to write a poem in honor of the many underappreciated women who had served in the Civil War. She took a pen and began writing. The words flowed from her heart.

> The women who went to the field, you say,
> The *women* who went to the field, and pray,
> What did they go for? just to be in the way!
> They'd not know the difference betwixt work
>   and play,
> What did they know about war anyway?
> What could they *do*?—of what use could they
>   be?
> They would scream at the sight of a gun,
>   don't you see?

Once Clara started writing she could not stop, and the poem went on for eighty-five more lines, describing the heroic work that so many women had accomplished.

"The Women Who Went To The Field" became an overnight sensation. Newspapers carried it from one end of the United States to the other, and lines from it became the mottoes for many branches of the Red Cross. The poem stirred a nation, although not enough to meet the next major disaster.

This time the disaster came in the form of a hurricane that roared up from the Caribbean and over the Sea Islands off South Carolina with the force of a freight train. The islands, which stretch one hundred miles along the coast of South Carolina, are low-lying. At first it was said that there were no survivors among their inhabitants. The wind had been so strong that it ripped the clothes off people's backs and wiped the islands completely clean of homes, crops, fences, and wharves. But slowly, pathetic stories of those who had in fact survived began to surface. Some of these survivors were badly bruised or had multiple broken bones, and children were found clinging to the dead bodies of their parents.

When she heard these stories of survivors, Clara set out immediately with Dr. Julian Hubbell to survey the damage. She found conditions on the islands as terrible as they had been described to her. She immediately sent off a request for funds from Congress and an appeal to the general population. What happened next appalled her. Congress refused to give the Sea Islanders any money. Instead they gave Clara the use of two small boats to get from island to island but offered no relief goods to load into them. To make matters worse, little money was raised through the national campaign for donations to meet the disaster. In fact, when donations were counted, they amounted to thirty thousand dollars, a single dollar for each man, woman, and child who now had to find a way to live on the storm-ravaged islands until yet unplanted crops could be harvested. Not only did Clara need to find a way to clothe them on that amount, but she also wanted to help the people meet medical needs and rebuild homes.

The reason for the poor response to the appeal, especially after the outpouring of support in response to the Johnstown flood, was obvious to Clara. The Sea Islanders were poor, rural, and black. Thirty-one years after the Emancipation Proclamation, most white Americans were simply not yet ready to open their hearts and wallets to help black people. Clara, whose first black friends had been the Sea Islanders she met while staying on the islands with her brother David, determined that she and the small team that joined her would do what they could, despite people's reticence to give.

The task was enormous, and Clara realized that the islanders would have to help themselves or they would never get back on their feet. There was little food to be distributed; it amounted to only a peck of hominy and a pound of pork for a family of seven. However, husbands and fathers who helped dig new drainage ditches all over the islands were given twice that amount of food for their families. And no one got any rations at all unless he planted a small vegetable garden. This proved quite a challenge, because the Sea Islanders were not used to growing their own vegetables in small plots. Before the hurricane they had raised high-quality cotton, worked in phosphate mines, and sold fish to make money.

Clara also set up a sewing room, much as she had done in Strasbourg during the Franco-Prussian War. The fabric for the sewing room arrived in the form of out-of-fashion ball gowns that rich women in the North sent down. The Sea Island women picked the seams of the garments, ironed the fabric, and remade it into practical clothes for themselves and their families.

Bit by bit, order was restored, and once the first crop of cabbages, lettuces, onions, peas, and potatoes was harvested, Clara and her team had to set about showing the island women how to prepare the vegetables. The Sea Islanders now had a better diet than before the hurricane, but that wasn't the only thing that had improved. Under the banner of the Red Cross, more than 245 miles of drainage ditches had been dug, 200,000 garments distributed, five tons of garden seed planted, and thousands of new homes built. Despite the risk of dysentery from the contaminated wells on the islands, not a single life had been lost since the hurricane itself rolled through.

By June 1894 Clara felt confident that the Sea Islanders were ready to take over things for themselves. Their gardens were bountiful and spirits high. Clara left the Sea Islands feeling very proud of what the Red Cross had been able to achieve with just one dollar per person.

Chapter 16

All Those It Was Sworn to Serve

Painful news awaited Clara upon her return to Washington. A young member of the New York chapter of the Red Cross named Sophia Williams had stirred up a lot of problems while Clara was away. Sophia was an outspoken and ambitious person, and she took aim at Clara's leadership of the organization and the way Clara did business. In her heart Clara knew that many of the criticisms had some truth to them. She had never required a lot of financial checks and balances, because she trusted those under her to spend the money wisely, as she did herself. This meant that twenty different members of the Red Cross were able to write checks on the organization's accounts, and Clara never asked to see their receipts. Although no one doubted that she had given a lot more money to the Red Cross than she had ever taken from it, there was no way to prove this. Sophia and her band of followers accused Clara of using the Red Cross to make herself rich and travel the world in comfort! And while nothing could have been further from the truth, many others began to question Clara's ways.

Another matter that bothered Clara's critics was the way Clara tended to dictate what the Red Cross would be involved with. Although she enjoyed and needed a team around her, she knew that someone had to be the leader with the right to tell the others what to do. But Sophia complained that a committee headed by some famous doctor would be a more fitting leadership structure for the Red Cross.

All the bickering tired Clara out. She was now seventy-three years old and wanted to live out the rest of her years in peace. She knew she had made mistakes. She also knew that the American Red Cross was like a child growing into adulthood. It had been her baby, and now it was getting too big for her to handle alone. Clara wrote in her diary that she would give up the leadership of the organization but not quite yet. She wanted to hold on a little longer to see it get a little bigger, a little more stable, and more widely recognized.

One thing Clara did not plan to do anymore was to travel on behalf of the Red Cross. It was therefore a great surprise to her when the United States Congress asked to see her. The meeting was over a problem that had been brewing for several years across the world in Armenia. The situation was complex, and from what Clara had read in the newspapers, it went like this. The Turkish people of the Ottoman empire were trying to take over the Armenians. The Turks were Muslims, and the Armenians were Christians. As a result, a bloody religious confrontation had arisen. At first the United States was not particularly interested in helping the Armenians, but after several American missionaries were killed by the Turks, the U.S. government's anger was aroused, and it began to watch the situation carefully.

By 1895 thousands of Armenians had been killed, and those who had survived were homeless and starving. Congress and the American people now thought that something should be done about the suffering of the Armenians. The problem was that the Turkish sultans would never allow Americans to bring in food and supplies to strengthen the people the Turks were trying to destroy. And that is why Congress called on Clara. Turkey was a member of the Red Cross and therefore would let Red Cross workers in. Since Clara was a famous figure, Congress asked if she would be willing to take American aid to Armenia.

Even though she was now seventy-four, Clara rose to the challenge. She asked Dr. Julian Hubbell and George Pullman, nephew of the famous railcar maker, to join her. On January 22, 1896, they set off on the long voyage to Europe. Once there, Clara stayed in Constantinople and directed the work of four teams that fanned out through the war-torn area.

The assignment proved to be an extremely difficult one for many reasons. The Muslims did not like the symbol of the Red Cross, so Clara had it painted over on all the tools and supplies and replaced with her initials, C. B. Money was also a headache beyond imagining. Clara wished that some of her detractors were there to try to work through the mess and keep perfect records. She, with the able assistance of George Pullman, dealt in Greek, Italian, Arabic, Kurdish, Turkish, and Armenian currencies, and even wax-sealed pouches of gold dust, which they entrusted to workers traveling through thief-infested regions.

While all of this was creating more than enough stress for Clara, she was receiving more criticism from home. As always, the Red Cross promised to help all those in need, regardless of race or religion. This meant that there were times when Clara's workers aided desperate Muslims as well as Christians. This incensed many Americans who had given money to help Christians, not to strengthen their enemies. Clara could see their point, but she remained steadfast. The Red Cross would falter if it did not help *all* those it was sworn to serve.

By the time she returned home to the United States in September 1896, Clara was exhausted from fending off criticism about the Red Cross and its international efforts. She had no idea that before too long she would be embarking on an even more politically charged international mission. This time it would take her only ninety miles off the coast of the United States, to Cuba.

Cuba, the small island nation to the south of Florida, was still ruled by Spain. While Clara had been away in Europe, the Cubans had risen up against their Spanish overlords. The Spanish soon squashed the rebellion and put harsh new laws into place. One of these new laws included rounding up all rebels, who were called *reconcentrados*, and putting them into concentration camps.

Over time the treatment of these men and women became more and more harsh, until in 1897 word reached the world that many of them were dying either from starvation or from lack of medical care. The newspapers kept the issue of the *reconcentrados* in front of the American public and called for the government to rescue the victims, some of whom were known to be Americans.

The United States government, on the other hand, was reluctant to act. After all, the Cubans were under Spanish rule, and helping them would mean risking the wrath of Spain. This policy was not good enough for some people, and one young politician named Theodore Roosevelt took matters into his own hands, recruiting a volunteer army to be ready to fight at a moment's notice. Since so many of the men he recruited were cowboys, they soon earned the nickname "Rough Riders."

Clara's heart, of course, went out to the imprisoned men, women, and children, and she ached for a way to help them. President McKinley, however, appeared to be doing little to resolve the issue of what the government should do, until Christmas 1897, when he finally came up with a plan. He proposed that a group called the Central Cuban Relief Committee be formed to solicit funds that would then be given to the Red Cross to supply aid to the *reconcentrados.* For his plan to be received with confidence, he appointed Clara Barton to personally take care of the relief operation.

Once again Clara was in the thick of things. She made preparations as quickly as she could and set sail south for Havana, Cuba. What she saw there shocked her. People in the concentration camps looked like skeletons with skin stretched over their bones. It was every bit as bad as Andersonville had been well over thirty years before. Clara paid visits to many Spanish officials to get the permission she needed to help the starving people. She was very careful not to talk politics with them but to stress the humanity of offering aid to starving citizens of their colony. There was no way to tell for sure, but the best estimate was that two hundred thousand of these people had died or were on the verge of death. Clara's arguments won the day, and she was allowed to take supplies to the *reconcentrados* and set up medical stations to treat the people.

The fragile relationship between Spain and America, however, was to blow up on February 15, 1898.

It was late at night, and Clara was doing some paperwork in a waterfront house when the table under her shook violently. She heard a deafening roar, and the double glass doors that overlooked Havana Harbor flew open. Out in the harbor an enormous ball of light flared into the air. Clara ran to the door to see what was happening as bells rang, whistles blew, and people started yelling and running.

One of Clara's assistants rushed out to see what had happened and came back with the awful news. The USS *Maine*, a sleek American battleship anchored in the harbor, had been blown up! Clara grabbed a bag of provisions and ran from the house. The survivors were all taken to the nearest hospital. Clara sat at their bedsides, listening to their stories and writing letters home for them. When dawn broke, 260 crewmen were pronounced dead or missing. No one knew just what had caused the explosion, but most Americans felt certain that the Spanish had blown it up to inflame the situation.

Clara went to great lengths to assure the Spanish that the Red Cross was not interested in who blew up the USS *Maine;* it was an international organization that offered relief regardless of political events.

Clara and her team quietly continued their work, setting up orphanages and soup kitchens in the fenced-off areas. When Senator Redfield Proctor arrived in Cuba to assess the situation, he was very impressed with the work the Red Cross was doing. He reported back to the Senate that Clara Barton and the Red Cross were doing the job the American people had sent them to do. He said:

> I have known and esteemed [Clara] for many years, but had not half appreciated her capability and devotion to her work. I specially looked into her business methods, fearing that here would be the greatest danger of mistake, that there might be want of system

> and waste and extravagance, but found she could teach me on these points.... In short I saw nothing to criticize, but everything to commend. The American people may be assured that their bounty will reach the sufferers with the least possible cost and in the best manner in every respect.

Clara was happy to read of the senator's report, which she hoped would calm some of the turmoil that still brewed around her. However, the strong and wealthy New York chapter of the Red Cross continued to stir up trouble for her, and in March Clara decided to make a quick trip back to Washington to quiet the rumors and also to charter a relief ship.

It proved to be the wrong time to leave Cuba. On April 25, President McKinley bowed to public hysteria and announced war on Spain. By then Clara had chartered the SS *State of Texas* and filled it with fourteen hundred tons of supplies for the *reconcentrados*. To her dismay, Congress ordered a naval blockade of Cuba. No ships were allowed in or out of the island. Clara was frustrated by this turn of events because the Treaty of Geneva covered only land areas. The Red Cross thus had no official recognition at sea to force one of its ships through a blockade.

Never one to give up, Clara instead sailed on the *State of Texas* to Tampa, Florida, where American troops were massing, and waited for the situation to change. She waited for two months. During this time the Red Cross members onboard the *State of Texas* filled their hours learning Spanish and collecting supplies. They also did something that turned many people against Clara. American troops were taking Spanish prisoners of war back to Tampa. Seeing that many of these soldiers were wounded, Clara and the Red Cross workers tended to their wounds and fed them. They did this with supplies that were supposed to be used for the *reconcentrados*. Clara knew she would be harshly judged for this action, but she felt that it was the right thing to do. After all, she could not get through the blockade to feed the Cubans, and the only people in need happened to be Spanish soldiers.

Finally, on June 20, 1898, Clara learned that the United States navy was leaving Tampa and heading for the Spanish fleet, which was patrolling off the coast of Santiago, Cuba. She applied for permission to sail with them, but when she did not get an answer back, she decided to join them anyway. It was her best chance at running the blockade.

On June 25, Clara was standing on the deck of the *State of Texas* when the coastline of Cuba appeared over the horizon. As the ship chugged closer, she heard the telltale gunfire of battle. The *State of Texas* pulled alongside one of the navy vessels so that Clara could find out what had happened.

Apparently some of the Rough Riders, who had been on board one of the ships, had landed and started fighting the Spanish in a series of skirmishes. The navy captain told Clara that there were many casualties. This was all she needed to hear. The Red Cross swung into action, and at the age of seventy-six, Clara found herself once again on a battlefield. She had never thought she would make gruel around a campfire again, and the memories of so many other battlefields flooded her mind as she did so.

This time, though, she was especially saddened because she felt that the entire war was the result of newspaper owners' whipping up public sentiment. She summed up her feelings in a letter to a friend:

> I am sorry for this war, but now that we are in it there is no way but to go through it. I never thought to see and take part in another war. It seems very strange that I should do so. Sometimes I almost think that it is not right, that too much of that kind of thing comes to me; but it is the last and must be met as it can be.

Clara had never stopped to think that rather than wars coming to her, she went to the wars!

Thankfully, the entire Spanish-American War lasted less than one hundred days. The Spanish surrendered on July 17, 1898, and a peace treaty was signed in Paris in December. As part of the peace treaty, Spain recognized Cuba's independence and agreed, under heavy pressure, to "sell" the Philippines, Puerto Rico, and the Pacific island of Guam to the United States.

Clara and the Red Cross had done what they could during the battle, but they did not have the manpower to be everywhere at once. The final count for what she considered a totally unnecessary war was more than 5,000 American soldiers dead from food poisoning, malaria, and yellow fever, plus the 379 who had died in the fighting.

When the war was over, Clara retreated to Glen Echo. She needed a break from the constant crowds. In the quiet of Glen Echo, she busied herself milking her Jersey cow, cleaning house, and writing a book on the work of the Red Cross. Upon her return from Cuba, her "enemies" within the Red Cross looked over every piece of paperwork she handed in, often making a fuss over a one- or two-dollar voucher that had not been recorded properly.

Clara was sure that she would never go to another battlefront, but two years after the Spanish-American War, another massive natural disaster drew her away from Glen Echo. On September 8, 1900, a huge hurricane engulfed the city of Galveston, Texas. The population of the city was thirty-eight thousand, and the first reports out of the area estimated that about six thousand of them—one out of every six or seven people in town—were dead. Many of them had been swept out to sea, while others lay in the rubble and wreckage.

Clara could imagine the scene, and she knew that the Red Cross could help bring order and dignity to those who were left behind. When the Pullman Company offered to get her to Galveston by train, she readily accepted its offer.

When Clara arrived in the city, she took her usual walking tour of the devastation. She recorded her first impressions in her journal.

> The streets are well nigh impassable, the animals largely drowned, the working force of men diminished, dazed and homeless. The men who had been fathers of the city, its business and its wealth, looked on aghast at their overwhelmed possessions, ruined homes, and worse than all, mourned their own dead.... Scores of persons came alive out of the wreckage with simply the band of a short or a nightdress held by its button about the neck.

Clara wrote about the smell, too. All over Galveston dead bodies were being burned on huge funeral pyres. Because the ground was too waterlogged to bury anyone, as soon as bodies were found, they were burned in the hope of preventing disease.

As usual, Clara was a shrewd observer of need, and she put out appeals for the things the survivors needed most: stoves, heaters, clothes, and seeds. Her Sea Island experience had taught her the importance of planting crops as soon as possible. Once the crops were harvested, food and money would start to flow into the devastated area. The crop farmers around Galveston were grateful to receive one and one-half million strawberry plants that thrived in the silty soil of the area. The plants bloomed by Christmas and were ready for picking in February.

When she returned to Washington, Clara was the special guest of President McKinley. The president praised her work in Texas and Cuba and signed a bill that gave the Red Cross a federal charter from Congress.

Later that year, on September 6, 1901, Clara was saddened by the news that President McKinley had been shot while attending the Pan-American Exposition in Buffalo, New York. McKinley died eight days later, on September 14. Clara recalled the assassinations of Abraham Lincoln and James Garfield, and now William McKinley had also been assassinated. She wondered how many other people were still alive who not only remembered but also personally knew each of the three slain presidents.

Nearing her eightieth birthday in December 1901, Clara began to wonder how much longer she would live. Most of her generation was gone, and she felt very much alone. Thinking that one day people might want to know a little about her life, she set to work writing an autobiography.

Chapter 17

The Woman Who Went to the Field

The internal wrangling at the Red Cross continued until a group under the influence of a woman named Mabel Boardman called for a public investigation of Clara Barton. This mortified Clara, but to her great relief all the charges made against her proved groundless and her reputation was restored. In 1902 members of the Red Cross elected Clara as their president for life.

But finally, in 1904, at the age of eighty-three, Clara decided it was time to retire from the Red Cross, and she resigned her position as president. In her farewell speech, she spoke about the future of the organization.

> Although its growth may seem to have been slow, it is to be remembered that it is not a shrub, or plant, to shoot up in the

> summer and wither in the frosts. The Red Cross is a part of us—it has come to stay—and like the sturdy oak, its spreading branches shall yet encompass and shelter the relief of the nation.

While Clara may have retired from the Red Cross, she certainly was not about to retire from life. Her great-nieces and -nephews were horrified to learn in 1910 that their eighty-eight-year-old Aunt Clara had accepted an invitation to speak in Chicago and had set off on the journey there alone. It was over a thousand miles to Chicago, and Clara refused help with her luggage, or any other aid normally extended to "old ladies." The woman who had led wagonloads of supplies into Civil War battles was not about to give up her independence!

When someone suggested that she might like a nap, Clara replied, "How can you insult one so young as I by asking her to rest in the middle of the afternoon? Are you in your right mind to ask *me* to rest?"

A journalist who came to Glen Echo found Clara on her hands and knees, hammering at a broken piece of sidewalk. Clara looked up at her and, noting the surprised look, retorted, "Well, my child, I should be very much ashamed if, after the life of hard work I have led, I had not learned how to wield a hammer."

But bit by bit Clara was slowing down. Her ninety-first birthday was a quiet affair, and soon after it, in January 1912, she came down with pneumonia. Her nephew Stephen and Dr. Hubbell remained at her side as she grew weaker. She hung on for three months. Then, on April 12, 1912, Clara Barton stirred herself one last time. She opened her eyes and murmured, "Let me go, let me go." Then she was gone.

In a strange coincidence, the woman who had been born on Christmas Day died on Good Friday.

Clara had left strict instructions for a simple funeral at North Oxford, Massachusetts. Stephen and Dr. Hubbell set about transporting her body back to her birthplace. They traveled by train but had to make a connection in New York, where they transferred the coffin from one station to the next in a covered wagon. When Dr. Hubbell told the driver that the coffin he was transporting contained the body of Clara Barton, tears welled in the man's eyes. "Why," he exclaimed, "my father was a Confederate soldier at the Battle of Antietam. He was wounded in the neck and was bleeding to death when Miss Barton found him on the battlefield and bound up his wounds in time to save his life."

Although many kind words were said at Clara's funeral service, in the numerous cards that arrived by mail, and in the articles that reported her death, the simple words of the wagon driver in New York would have been praise enough for Clara.

She was the woman who went to the field. Her desire was to help any soldier, Confederate or Union, black or white, Spanish or American, Christian or Muslim. She fought hard to impart this vision to the American Red Cross, and she forever shaped its future and, with it, the future of millions of people around the globe.

Bibliography

Boylston, Helen Dore. *Clara Barton: Founder of the American Red Cross.* Random House, 1955.

Hamilton, Leni. *Clara Barton: Founder, American Red Cross.* Chelsea House Publishers, 1988.

Pollard, Michael. *The Red Cross and the Red Crescent.* New Discovery Books, 1994.

Pryor, Elizabeth Brown. *Clara Barton: Professional Angel.* University of Pennsylvania Press, 1987.

Ross, Ishbel. *Angel of the Battlefield: The Life of Clara Barton.* Harper & Brothers Publishers, 1956.

Savage, Douglas J. *Civil War Medicine.* Chelsea House Publishers, 2000.

Whitelaw, Nancy. *Clara Barton: Civil War Nurse.* Enslow Publishers, 1997.

About the Authors

Janet and Geoff Benge are a husband and wife writing team with more than thirty years of writing experience. Janet is a former elementary school teacher. Geoff holds a degree in history. Originally from New Zealand, the Benges spent ten years serving with Youth With A Mission. They have two daughters, Laura and Shannon, and an adopted son, Lito. They make their home in the Orlando, Florida, area.